Fr
Hope

Jesse Adams

From Love to Hope copyright © 2023
Jesse Adams

All rights reserved.

No part of this publication may be reproduced, distributed, or transmitted in any form or by any means, including photocopying, recording, or other electronic or mechanical methods, without the prior written permission of the author, except in the case of brief quotations embodied in critical reviews and certain other noncommercial uses permitted by copyright law. Piracy of copyrighted material is a criminal offense.

This book is independently published.

Cover design by Jesse Adams

ISBN: 9798862036442

This book is dedicated to those who believed in me when I couldn't believe in myself—my friends, family, and coworkers.

Thank you for keeping me grounded.

Contents

Dear Reader	1
Chapter 1: Falling in Love	3
Chapter 2: Being in Love	33
Chapter 3: The Breakup	63
Chapter 4: Depression	93
Chapter 5: Healing and Hope	123

Dear Reader,

As you hold this book in your hands and embark on a journey through its pages, I want to share with you the heart and soul behind the words you are about to encounter. This poetry collection is not just ink on paper; it is a reflection of the real, raw emotions coursing through my veins, a testament to the battles I've fought within my mind.

You may notice a recurring theme, a pattern of metaphors and emotions that may appear repetitive at first glance. This repetition is not a result of laziness or a lack of creativity; instead, it is a conscious choice I made to lay bare the innermost workings of my heart and mind.

I suffer from OCD and depression, two relentless companions that have shadowed my life. When the darkness of depression descends upon me, my thoughts and emotions become trapped in a cycle of repetition, like a broken record repeatedly playing the same tune. It's as if my mind is stuck in quicksand, struggling to break free.

Through this book, I aim to provide you with an unfiltered glimpse into the chaos and beauty of my inner world. The repetitive metaphors and themes you encounter mirror these conditions' persistent and intrusive nature. They are a testament to the authenticity of the emotions I've experienced, the highs and lows of falling in love, the ecstasy of being in love, the crushing weight of heartbreak, the abyss of depression, and the slow, arduous journey toward healing.

I did not want to present a polished, sanitized version of myself. Instead, I chose to showcase the real me—the one who grapples with the demons of mental illness and emerges, sometimes battered but always resilient, on the other side. This book of vulnerability is about letting you see the cracks and imperfections and celebrating the strength that arises from confronting and embracing them.

As you turn the pages, I hope you find solace in the shared human experience of love, loss, and the pursuit of healing. May you discover that even amid repetition and turmoil, a profound beauty exists—a testament to the enduring spirit within us all.

Thank you for embarking on this journey with me. I hope that by the end, we both emerge stronger, more understanding, and more connected in our shared humanity.

With heartfelt gratitude,

Jesse

Chapter 1
Falling in Love

"Carnival of Dreams"

In carousel's gentle twirl, their bond hath grown,
A journey unfurling, like love's bard's sweetest tone.
Beneath the carnival's bright lights, amid joyful sound,
Their love tale danced, in merriment profound.

Hand in hand, they strolled with grace so fine,
Soul to soul, hearts entwined, in love's design.
Within the carnival's enchantment, love found space,
Its sweet allure, in their tender, warm embrace.

Bold and open-hearted, love took center stage,
In the carnival's marvel, they'd engage.
Love's fragrance filled the air, a soaring flight,
A tapestry of affection, woven pure and bright.

Their love story, a joyful, heartwarming ride,
A journey through dreams, side by side.
In the heart of the carnival, their eternal place,
A love-filled voyage, brimming with joy and grace.

"Starry Canvas"

Upon the dark canvas, love's story takes flight,
Beneath night's shroud, in the celestial night.
The artist, stars' gentle gleam in his quiver,
Two hearts, intertwined, in a timeless river.

He gazes upon her, night's wondrous embrace,
Her eyes, dream-filled orbs, in that tranquil space.
Her gaze, a repository of tales to amass,
As love's odyssey begins, in shadows cast.

The canvas, expansive, guided by each bright star,
Emotions laid bare, no distance too far.
Touches and whispers, an artwork sublime,
Painting emotions, in the gallery of time.

The night sky bears witness to love's sweet refrain,
Constellations, storytellers, the universe's domain.
Hearts intertwined, like stars' endless flight,
A journey through cosmos, love's radiant light.

"Moonlit Promises"

Beneath the moon's soft, argent gleam,
Two souls entwined, as in a cherished dream.
Their hearts bared to the cosmic expanse,
Bound by a love, an unshakable stance.

In the hush of the night, their pledge was spun,
A sacred union, a promise begun.
Moonlit vows, whispered from above,
A love ordained to flourish, a tale of true love.

Beneath the starry, endless, night-kissed sky,
Their vows resounded, reaching heavens high.
A love built to withstand, to everlast,
Guided by the moon's unwavering cast.

They vowed to soar through love's limitless flight,
Under the vigilant, guiding light.
In the embrace of vows, they found their way,
A love destined to blossom, eternally to stay.

"Whispering Breeze"

In the heart's free flight, a tale unwinds,
Beneath the moon's soft glow, their destiny finds.
A man and woman, fate's chosen decree,
Bound by love's force, as all could plainly see.

His heart, a leaf afloat in night's gentle breeze,
In quiet pursuit of her, under moonlight's ease.
Fate's unseen waltz, a chance rendezvous,
Ignites a flame, a passion both felt true.

Her presence, a murmur in the wind's tender sway,
Stirs emotions they can't keep at bay.
Fate's hand, in destiny's cosmic dance,
Weaves a love fleeting at first glance.

Defying time's grasp, its unjust rule,
Their universe whirls, a celestial duel.
In the cosmic ballet of souls, as one,
Their love's journey has just begun.

The path ahead, a mystery untold,
Yet in this moment, doubt and fear are cajoled.
The breeze's soft whisper, a secret key,
To a love story etched in destiny's decree.

"Garden of Hearts"

In the garden of love's pure embrace,
Two hearts entwined, a passionate chase.
Each moment, a blossom in love's fertile ground,
Their story unfolded, a flower unbound.

Their love, a garden of colors so vast,
Each bloom a memory, in love's tender cast.
With gentle hands, they tended their devotion,
Nurturing it with shared moments, a heartfelt potion.

Beneath the sun's embrace and the moon's soft art,
Their love flourished, finding its place, a sacred part.
In this garden, emotions grew wild and free,
A sanctuary of love, where hearts danced in glee.

With every petal, a tale was unfurled,
A love beyond riches, in a material world.
Their heart's garden, in perpetual bloom,
A sanctuary of love, a fragrant, sacred room.

"Beneath the Oak"

Two hearts found solace, their spirits unchained,
In this tranquil haven, where secrets gently rained.
A love story grew, its roots went deep,
As whispered confessions their hearts did keep.

The oak, a silent sentinel, their witness there,
As souls unveiled, like birdsong in the air.
Their laughter danced among rustling leaves,
A bond blossoming beneath the forest's eaves.

In the shadow of those wise and mighty boughs,
A sanctuary of trust, where love allows.
Their story woven in the oak's warm embrace,
A haven of connection, their hearts' sacred space.

The oak, a towering sage, steadfast and true,
Beheld their love beneath the endless blue.
Their memories entwined in nature's art,
A love story blooming, stitched in their heart.

In nature's tender brush, their love unfurled,
A tale of devotion beneath the ancient oak, their world.

"Symphony of Smiles"

In a realm of joy, where mirth conducts the play,
Two hearts dance, their bond in a splendid array.
Never letting go, they move as one,
Smiles like musical notes in the radiant sun.

Their love tale unfolds with a harmonious line,
Laughter and giggles, a love so fine.
In this rhythm of bliss, they find their stance,
Smiles composing the music, life's sweetest dance.

A duet of hearts, an exquisite pair,
From love's initial note to the final prayer.
Their symphony of smiles, free from despair,
In each other's presence, a bond beyond compare.

In this melody of joy, they gracefully soar,
Their love story, a symphony to adore.
Forged from moments they both embrace,
In life's grand orchestra, they've found their place.

Their hearts in the ensemble, they take their part,
A symphony of smiles, touching every heart.
In this rare symphony, their love does gleam,
A symphony of smiles, their eternal theme.

"Crimson Sunsets"

The sky ablaze in crimson and gold,
Two hearts entwined as the sun's tale unfolds.
Love's soft flames in twilight's warm hold,
Colors harmonize, memories of love, ever bold.

Hand in hand, they greet the sun's descent,
Passion and warmth, in love's sweet event.
Their hearts fearless, bold, and true,
In sunsets, their love's tale anew.

Beneath the sun's fond adieu,
A canvas of affection, love's debut.
In twilight's caress, they find their way,
Embracing each moment, come what may.

Their love, a truth that time secures,
Crimson sunsets etch love's contours.
Day yields to night's tender flight,
Their love's radiant glow, an eternal light.

"Love's Lighthouse"

In the radiant glow of love's own tower,
They found their path, an eternal hour.
Their hearts akin to sailors on the main,
A love story inked in eternity's domain.

With each sweep of the light, their love took flight,
Love's lighthouse, a guide through day and night.
In its tender embrace, they chose to reside,
A bond unbreakable, on love's steady tide.

When the light pierces the darkest abyss,
Their love sparks, a beacon's eternal kiss.
In its warm embrace, they've built their dome,
A love story anchored in the lighthouse's home.

Their love, a beacon, steadfast and true,
Through tempests and calm, they together grew.
Guided by the light, their hearts agleam,
A love story everlasting, a poet's dream.

"Lullaby of Love"

The lullaby of love, an art so soothing,
Bringing peace and solace, hearts softly moving.
A melody of comfort and joy it imparts,
Their sacred bond, where the lullaby starts.

In whispers and tender embraces, they find grace,
Serenity found in love's warm embrace.
In the lullaby's tender and soothing sway,
Worries dissolve in love's gentle display.

Their love tale woven in this tranquil song,
A melody of emotions where they both belong.
As the lullaby plays, spirits mend and blend,
A harmonious journey without an end.

In love's embrace, they find their way,
Guiding them through each brand-new day.
Their love, a lullaby, calming every soul,
A symphony of emotions making them whole.

In the rhythm of their love story's sweet tune,
Deep and rich, beneath the gentle moon.

"Melody of Laughter"

Laughter, the melodious essence of hearts so true,
A chorus of joy where love finds its debut.
Notes of mirth in a sweet and harmonious suite,
A love story woven in laughter's rhythmic beat.

With every shared laugh, their bond does grow,
In the cadence of merriment, love's fervor does flow.
A symphony of emotions, unrestrained and free,
In their laughter's melody, love's song does decree.

As laughter binds their souls in pure delight,
A love story twirls in the starry night's light.
In the laughter's melody, love's magic is found,
A bond to endure life's challenges, unbound.

Their love, a harmonious melody's warm embrace,
In the joyful refrain, they find a special place.
A love story composed, devoid of sorrow's stain,
In laughter's sweet melody, their hearts remain.

"Candlelit Conversations"

Beneath the gentle flicker of a candle's flame,
They shared their tales, free from any blame.
Profound conversations, secrets unconfined,
Their bond was unbreakable, as the candlelight shined.

Each flicker spoke truths, their moment agleam,
Sealing their hearts in a luminous stream.
Dreams, desires, hopes set ablaze,
In the fire's warmth, their love's enduring phase.

Candles bore witness as words took their flight,
Illuminating souls through the tranquil night.
In whispered discourse, bonds closely sewn,
Hearts and thoughts are forever known.

A dance of words in the candle's tender trace,
Their love story etched in that soft-lit space.
Candlelit conversations, trust interlace,
In the gentle illumination, love found its place.

"Silhouette of Love"

In love's gentle shadow, their figures take flight,
Two souls entwined, no need for the night.
Their love tale is cast in shadows so fine,
A timeless narrative, life's bounds they outshine.

With every tender touch, their shapes align,
A love story woven where limits entwine.
In the silhouette's warm and tender grace,
Their hearts blend, no challenge they face.

No distance, no trial their bond shall forsake,
As their silhouettes dance in twilight's wake.
In the setting sun's hue, they find their space,
A love's connection, no darkness can erase.

A love that never fades, like a ceaseless parade,
In the shadows' whispers, their story displayed.
A love destined to forever spin,
In love's silhouettes, their hearts will win.

"Starlit Whispers"

Beneath the starry canvas of midnight's deep blue,
Two souls intertwined, love's radiant debut.
In the murmurs of stars, their thoughts took flight,
A love story etched on the Milky Way, pure and bright.

With every twinkling star in the celestial sea,
They exchanged secrets, wild and free.
In the language of constellations, they found their own,
A bond beyond words, uniquely known.

As stars whispered secrets in night's fond caress,
Their love story unfurled, a tale of finesse.
Star whispers resonated in the cosmic vast,
An unbreakable connection, a cosmic love amassed.

Their hearts attuned to the universe's grand design,
A love story shimmering, eternally divine.
In the starlit whispers of night's sweet terrain,
Their souls discovered solace, love's eternal reign.

"Harbor of Hearts"

They discovered a harbor of hearts, a love unrestrained,
In each other's tender embrace, where love's fire remained.
A love story crafted on trust's steadfast ground,
With every heartbeat, a harmonious sound.

In the refuge of their shared time, they would thrive,
A love unyielding, as hearts came alive.
No storm, no tempest could their bond ever sever,
Their love's story etched in their united endeavor.

When life's tempests raged, their love stood tall,
A sanctuary amidst chaos, an unwavering wall.
In the midst of turmoil, they would not part,
A refuge from the storm, forever in their heart.

As love's tides clashed, their hearts would guide,
Like a lighthouse of hope, unwavering beside.
An unbreakable beacon, through the darkest night,
Their love would persist, an eternal, radiant light.

"Eternal Duet"

Two birds soared over the endless azure sea,
Their wings entwined in a dance wild and free.
A duet of souls, a symphony's sweet start,
A love story commences where music imparts.

With each tender note, their love took its flight,
A melody of emotions, pure and bright.
Side by side, on this journey they'd embark,
Their love's sweet song echoed through the dark.

Through tempestuous winds and clear blue days,
They harmonized their hearts' endless ballet.
Their duet was painted on the azure dome,
Love found its place, a sanctuary to call home.

A shared melody, their souls forever twined,
An eternal duet, their spirits combined.
In love's boundless skies, they'll forever remain,
Their harmonious souls, an unending refrain.

"Sculpting Memories"

Their love, a sculptor's opus, profound and deep,
A journey of emotions, their hearts' secrets to keep.
From tender touches to whispers, so discreet,
They shaped memories together, a love complete.

Like artisans of clay, with skill and grace,
They molded moments, time couldn't erase.
In the river of time, their love took shape,
As memories bloomed, hearts couldn't escape.

Their tale etched in the clay's intricate line,
A sculpture of emotions, love so fine.
A life's work, this enduring art,
From gentle caresses to words that impart.

Each memory sculpted with meticulous care,
Every moment cherished, love's vibrant flare.
Their love story, a masterpiece in time,
One of a kind, memories forever entwined.

Sculpting memories that forever bind,
Their love's enduring legacy, one of a kind.

"Ink of Affection"

Their love, an unfathomable inkwell's embrace,
A boundless sea where affection finds its place.
Each drop of love, a river flowing wild and free,
In whispered words, their hearts found harmony.

In every line they penned, a love story's birth,
With each passionate stroke, ink flowed with mirth.
Pages filled with tales of joy and sweet delight,
Their bond grew stronger day and night.

In love's exquisite script, their tale unfurled,
Ink flowed through ages as life's story swirled.
Laughter, tears, and moments cherished dear,
In every verse, their hearts whisper clear.

A testament to love, unwavering and vast,
Their masterpiece of love, an eternal cast.
Written with the ink of hearts forever true,
Their love endures, forever fresh and anew.

In the chapters of their life, love shall reside,
A tale of two hearts, forever, side by side.

"Uncharted Constellations"

Amidst the night, they danced a cosmic ballet,
Guided by constellations in starlight's grand display.
Their love story entwined in the celestial unknown,
A cosmic connection, entirely their own.

With each twinkle in the endless sky,
They waltzed through galaxies, soaring high.
Constellations formed from their laughter and sighs,
A bond etched in stardust, a love that never dies.

They traced the patterns of the bright galaxies,
Found a love that fit, so harmoniously.
In an uncharted constellation, they'd uncover,
A love boundless, profound, and forever.

Their tale written in the stars' proclamation,
A connection as boundless as cosmic creation.
A tapestry woven in love's grand design,
A story destined in the universe's elegant sign.

"Waves of Serenity"

By the tranquil shore, their love did unfurl,
As gentle waves embraced them, a loving swirl.
Their hearts danced to the ocean's rhythmic grace,
A love story unfolding at a serene pace.

With each ebb and flow, their love took flight,
In the rhythm of the waves, a connection so right.
Their souls converged in the sands' tender meet,
A love story written where land and sea greet.

As the sea whispered secrets to the winds' soft hum,
Their love journey commenced, their hearts overcome.
Cradled by the calm waves, love's voyage did start,
A symphony of emotions where love played its part.

In the shoreline's tender kiss, they found pure bliss,
A love story to forever reminisce.
With every wave's gentle caress, they would mend,
A love story with no ending, that would eternally transcend.

"Autumn's Embrace"

In autumn's tender grasp, love came alive,
Colors of passion adorned where they'd arrive.
Their love story etched in leaves' graceful fall,
A connection profound, witnessed by time's call.

Their love grew more potent, beyond compare,
In the season's warm embrace, hearts took to the air.
A tale of love with chapters yet to be spun,
In autumn's tender hug, a union had begun.

As leaves danced upon the breeze, love soared high,
A tapestry of emotions, painting the sky.
In the golden grace of autumn's tender whirl,
A love story unfurled, in nature's grand unfurl.

Their love, like leaves, changed with the season's rhyme,
Defying reason, transcending time.
Entwined hearts, in perfect symphony,
Eternally designed, their love's melody.

"Harmony of Hands"

In the harmony of their hands, love's story did weave,
Fingers entwined, a tale of hearts that believe.
Guided by their touch, on a path so clear,
Their love story whispered, in every hand they held near.

With each tender caress and firm embrace,
Their love grew in strength under the moon's soft grace.
Time's futile grasp, their hearts in unity,
A love story unfolding with perfect continuity.

Beneath the moon's gentle, silvery sheen,
Their love blossomed, a celestial scene.
In the harmony of hands, their spirits took flight,
A love story tender and bright, in the soft moonlight.

Their love symphony, both gentle and grand,
Played in the union of every hand in hand.
In the harmonious connection, they did stand,
A love story flourishing, forever hand in hand.

"Sunrise Embrace"

In tender dawn's embrace, love's light did gleam,
Two souls awakened to a love like a dream.
Welcomed by the sun's gentle, golden kiss,
Their love story bloomed in nature's sweet abyss.

With every ray that graced the lofty sky,
Their love soared high, like birds in the morning's sigh.
The sunrise bore witness to their hearts' delight,
A passion's tale, a love unburdened and bright.

As golden fingers brushed their tender skin,
They felt the magic of love deep within.
Love at first sight, in morning's warm grace,
In the sunrise's tender hold, they found their place.

Their souls warmed by the touch of early light,
A love to withstand all trials, steadfast and right.
In the glow of dawn, their passion took flight,
A story painted in the soft morning light.

"Universe in Her Eye"

In the space within her eyes, his odyssey commenced,
Galaxies of emotions, in hues so finely nuanced.
Her gaze held enigmas, desires yet to uncover,
A love story, hidden within, their hearts would discover.

With every blink, a narrative softly unrolled,
A love so vast it enveloped their world.
In the constellations of her eyes, he'd trace,
A connection profound, where their souls found their place.

As he delved into the depths of her soulful stare,
A love unwavering through life's intricate affair.
Within the realm of her eye, he'd explore,
A love story bound to endure, forevermore.

Her eyes, mirrors of love's untamed grace,
A story framed within his heart's embrace.
In the universe within her gaze's allure,
Love's secrets concealed, a journey to heart's pure.

With her eyes as their guide, souls soared high,
A love story painted on the canvas of the endless sky.

"Raindrop Serenade"

Their love, a duet in soft rain's fond caress,
Every drop, a note, a love story to profess.
Raindrops descend in perfect, rhythmic chime,
Their love's melody sung in nature's prime.

Amidst the falling rain, their bond fortified,
A symphony of emotions, side by side.
Raindrops kissed their skin, whispers so sweet,
A serenade of love, an intimate feat.

As raindrops touched their heads with gentle grace,
Their hearts heard nature's voice, a tender embrace.
In the rain's touch, their love took its flight,
A melody that would linger through the night.

A chorus of emotions, raindrops unfurled,
In this nameless world, their passion swirled.
Their story composed, in the rain's warm hold,
In every drop's dance, their love story was told.

"Silent Echoes"

In the silence, their hearts discovered a voice,
A language unspoken, a connection, their ultimate choice.
Their love story echoed in the stillness of the night,
A bond more potent than words, pure and bright.

As silence enveloped them, their souls drew near,
True feelings exchanged, no need for words to adhere.
In those tranquil moments, their world was unfurled,
A love story unveiled, as the night gently swirled.

When words fell short, their hearts knew the way,
Expressing more than words in their quiet ballet.
Feelings echoed in the hush, whispers of care,
A love beyond spoken language, a love beyond compare.

Their connection thrived in the grace of the silent hour,
A love story etched in each tranquil bower.
In the realm of the unspoken, their love found its voice,
A love that flourished in the stillness, their ultimate choice.

"Enchanted Waltz"

Amidst the moon's whispers, tender and low,
A dance unfurled, hearts in a radiant glow.
Two souls enchanted by love's intricate plan,
In an enchanting waltz, their dreams began.

He held her close, the universe in her gaze,
Their rhythm was gentle, in love's timeless maze.
Through ages, they waltzed, side by side,
Love's melody was their eternal guide.

With each graceful turn, their spirits took flight,
In love's grand hall beneath the starry night.
A dance that spoke where words couldn't thread,
A bond, a masterpiece, in every step they spread.

Their waltz narrated a tale in each graceful swirl,
A connection deepening with each twirl.
Two souls swaying in cosmic embrace,
Love's dance immortal in their sacred space.

"Whispers on the Wind"

Whispers of confession, shared between just two,
Their love story carried by the breeze, ever true.
A symphony of words that erased their hearts' unease,
With each breath of wind, their bond found its keys.

In the rustling leaves, their emotions took flight,
Like secrets unveiled, love's story shone so bright.
Their love, a whisper to the world, unfurled,
The wind, their confidant, as emotions swirled.

Their secrets, like petals, soft and pure,
In the language of the wind, they felt secure.
No need for pretense; their love was voiced and clear,
In the whispers of the wind, they held dear.

A tale so sweet, on the wind it soared,
Their love story in every heartbeat was adored.
Carried by the currents, forevermore,
A story of love they both eternally wore.

"Infinite Horizons"

Hand in hand, they strolled, eyes fixed on the distant shore,
Endless horizons beckoned, love's voyage they'd explore.
Their hearts beat to the rhythm of the uncharted sea,
A love story destined to bloom, for all eyes to see.

With each stride toward the boundless, endless blue,
Promises of the future held, love pure and true.
In the vast expanse, their love would thrive and soar,
A journey of connection, forever to implore.

They gazed at the limitless skies above,
A union unwavering, built on trust and love.
Infinite horizons awaited their eager exploration,
A love story enduring, their hearts' dedication.

Through life's myriad turns, their bond held tight,
Love's guiding star through the darkest night.
In the realm of boundless horizons, they'd find,
A love that blossomed with each moment, forever entwined.

Chapter 2
Being in Love

"Unwritten Poetry"

In the realm of the unseen, a tale unfolds,
A world of emotions, where love dearly holds.
Invisible as the air we breathe, a bond unique,
Their love story, in silence, beautifully speaks.

With every gaze and whispered vow,
Their love deepens, unspoken but somehow;
In this wordless realm, their hearts align,
A love story meant to eternally shine.

As the ages gracefully turn and bend,
Their love's tapestry in this realm transcends.
In the poetry of the unspoken, they find their grace,
A love infinite, an enduring embrace.

An unwritten sonnet, in clarity and splendor,
A connection beyond words, so tender.
In the world yet unveiled, their love remains free,
A story of love's sweet, silent mystery.

"Secret Garden of Love"

In the hidden garden, love's tender vine,
Their hearts entwined, a sacred design,
A love tale flourished in secrets well-kept,
A sanctuary cherished, where dreams softly wept.

With each step through the garden gate's embrace,
Their bond grew steadfast, a profound grace,
In this hidden haven, they found their release,
Love is deeply rooted, never to decrease.

Whispers of blossoms in the gentle breeze,
Carried love's fragrance with such ease,
In the garden's secrecy, they found their place,
A tale of devotion, time cannot efface.

Love's treasure, concealed among the blooms,
In the garden's embrace, eternally looms,
In this sanctuary of devotion's seat,
Their story, in hushed tones, is pure and complete.

"Captured Moments"

In the tapestry of time, their moments were portrayed,
Captured memories, in love's embrace, they swayed,
Their story painted in photographs, vivid and near,
Precious moments that to their hearts drew near.

With every heartbeat's rhythm, their connection did flower,
A mosaic of memories, each one a cherished hour,
In the gallery of time, their smiles held sway,
A love story depicted day by day.

As pages gracefully turned, memories took flight,
A tapestry of moments, in laughter and light,
In the chronicle of time, their tale was spun,
A love preserved in memory, two hearts as one.

The tapestry of time, their love it enshrined,
A collection of moments, forever combined,
A testament to a love that radiates its light,
In the snapshots of life, their journey takes flight.

In the mosaic of memories, love's seeds were sown,
An affectionate bond in their hearts, fully known,
With every click and snap, the story continued to grow,
In captured moments, love's beauty is on full show.

"Serenading Sunrises"

With the sun's first kiss, their love's tale began,
A new day's promise, a love story's gentle span.
Morning's embrace, their hearts found their tune,
Love's canvas painted with the sunrise's boon.

As the sun graced the heavens, their bond grew bold,
No need for words or stories of old.
In the morning's light, their spirits aligned,
Their love story, like the dawn, is forever enshrined.

With each new daybreak, their love took its flight,
Bold hues of affection, morning to night.
With the sun's rise, their love endlessly gleamed,
A story of hope and light, like a cherished dream.

Their journey, as certain as the sun's ascent,
A love pure and strong, unwavering and unspent.
In the sunrise's glow, their connection would endeavor,
A love story, bonded forever and ever.

"Echoes of Laughter"

In echoes of laughter, their souls took flight,
A symphony of joy, from morning to night.
Their laughter, a melody that filled the air,
A love story composed with laughter's flair.

With shared jokes and playful teases so sweet,
Their connection deepened, hearts in harmonious beat.
In echoes of laughter, their bond was clear,
A unity of souls, drawing them near.

Their laughter resonated through time and space,
A bridge between hearts, a warm embrace.
In the echoes of laughter, their path they'd find,
A love story enriched, in every laugh, entwined.

Their love, a chorus of giggles and glee,
A connection that set their spirits free.
In laughter's embrace, their journey took wing,
A love story woven into every joyful ring.

"Symphony of Senses"

In a world where hearts unite, a symphony unfolds,
Sensations bloom in every glance their story holds,
Love's overture commences, time they won't efface,
A melody of caresses, a dance of tender grace.

Fingers strum like strings in an orchestral delight,
Unveiling in their embrace, love's tender flight,
Aroma of memories lingers in the scented air,
A love profound and subtle, beyond compare.

With each beat's cadence, the symphony takes wing,
Eyes meet like dancers in a passionate fling,
No words can truly capture the dance they share,
A smile that speaks volumes, a love story rare.

Gentle hands conduct this symphony so true,
Awakening every sense in the night's soft hue,
Love's crescendo rising like a guiding star,
Two hearts intertwined eternally, no matter how near or far.

"Euphoria's Dance"

In Euphoria's tender grasp, they found their sway,
Two souls in a waltz, hearts leading the way.
Their love tale flowed with rhythms so profound,
Spirits alive and dancing, love unbound.

With each step upon Euphoria's enchanted floor,
Their connection deepened, seeking to explore.
Hearts taking flight, emotions ever so bright,
A symphony of love in the dancing night.

As they twirled and waltzed, laughter would arise,
A love story composed in each dance's surprise.
In Euphoria's embrace, they found their special way,
A bond that would flourish, come what may.

Their love, timeless, tender, and sure,
In the enchantment of the dance floor's allure.
A love tale unveiled in endless grace,
In Euphoria's sweet embrace, their love found its place.

"Heartbeat Symphony"

Symphony of heartbeats, a love story's grand start,
In each pulse's lively dance, they'd find their heart.
Two souls entwined beneath the moon's bright glance,
Their love story unfolds in each rhythmic advance.

With each heartbeat's cadence, their bond takes the lead,
A rhythm of love, a dance born of need.
In the symphony of heartbeats, their love plants a seed,
A connection unbroken, a pure love indeed.

As their heartbeats entwine, a harmonious grace,
A melody of love in this unique embrace.
In the rhythm of their hearts, love finds its place,
A connection eternal, a warm, loving base.

Their love story, a symphony, pure and true,
A union of souls, forever they grew.
In the symphony of heartbeats, their love would renew,
A story of love composed in perfect harmony, just for the two.

"Tapestry of Affection"

In the tapestry of love, feelings take root,
No need for pretense, in each other they're astute,
Their hearts, like threads, weave patterns with grace,
A love story nurtured in moments, an enduring embrace.

With every glance, with every word they exchange,
Their bond deepens, love's endless range,
In the tapestry of affection, they chart their way,
A connection forged, both night and day.

Threads of their love, in vibrant display,
A love forever woven, come what may,
In the tapestry of affection, spirits thrive,
A love story to cherish and keep alive.

Every thread of love, colors so bright,
Their hearts entwined from dawn to night,
A connection crafted with hands so fair,
In this tapestry of affection, a love story they declare.

"Scented Memories"

In fragrant memories, their love finds its place,
Scented moments where hearts beautifully trace.
Their story lingers in each sweet perfume,
A bond so strong, it can dispel any gloom.

With every scent that fills the breeze,
They're transported to moments that put their hearts at ease.
In fragrances' embrace, their spirits take flight,
A connection that stands the test of day and night.

Scents paint memories, vivid and so true,
Their love story echoes, forever anew.
In fragrant memories, their hearts find delight,
An unbroken bond, a love shining bright.

Their love, a symphony of fragrances so clear,
A story cherished from year to year.
A tale that time can never efface,
Preserved in each aromatic embrace.

"Colors of Passion"

In autumn's gentle touch, amor unfurled,
Hues of ardor adorned their secret world.
Their tale engraved in leaves' serene descent,
A union profound, by time's event.

Their love burgeoned, unparalleled and rare,
Within the season's grasp, hearts filled the air.
A narrative of love, its pages yet to inscribe,
In autumn's tender clasp, a dulcet bribe.

As leaves pirouetted on zephyr's flight,
A tapestry of sentiments took its height.
In the golden elegance of autumn's gentle whirl,
A love saga blossomed, in nature's pearl.

Their love, akin to leaves, changed with each rhyme,
Defying reason, transcending the climb.
Entangled hearts, in perfect consonance,
Eternally ordained, love's melodious dance.

"Sunset Strolls"

Beneath the setting sun's ardent embrace,
They strolled, entwined, in love's eternal chase,
Their footsteps carving tales, time can't efface,
A love, a masterpiece, in this tranquil space.

With each step, their love's horizon would expand,
As daylight waned, they'd stand, hand in hand,
In the quiet sunset's grasp, forever planned,
A love story woven in the warm, golden sand.

Under the tender sun's waning light,
Their love's odyssey sailed, an endless flight,
In the hush of the twilight's tender glow,
Their bond grew firmer, a radiant flow.

Their love, a sunset walk through life's vast plain,
A journey of hearts, where memories remain,
In the tranquil embrace of night's sweet reign,
A love story flourished, its eternal refrain.

"Whispered Promises"

In whispers of vows, their future took its flight,
Love's essence transformed in the softest light.
Their words held dreams of what was yet to be,
A love tale inscribed in vows, wild and free.

Their connection deepened, akin to stone's embrace,
Trust thrived unwavering in love's sacred space.
An unbreakable bond, no obstacles in sight,
Their words, like trust's wings, took their flight.

As they erected a steadfast, just foundation,
In the whisper of vows, hearts found salvation.
A love story predestined, potent, and distinct,
In promises exchanged, love's words are succinct.

Their love, a symphony of vows in the air,
Promises interwoven, beyond compare.
Their souls found their purpose in this sacred pledge,
A love tale sealed by vows, an eternal edge.

"Enchanted Trails"

Upon enchanting trails, hand in hand they'd roam,
Exploring the world, love their cherished home.
A vast journey unfolds in each footfall they stride,
In their wake, a love tale, nowhere to hide.

Destiny, it appears, bound their hearts as one,
Upon these captivating paths, their union begun.
With every step they took, love's flame burned bright,
A passion's seed sown, taking boundless flight.

Amidst nature's embrace, their love took root,
As they wandered, their souls began to compute.
Whispers of love in every heart's soft cadence,
On enchanting paths, a love's sweet resonance.

Nature's enchantment elevated their spirits high,
A love saga unfurled beneath the open sky.
Their love, a map of cherished memories unfurled,
In nature's marvels, they'd discover the world.

On enchanting paths, where hearts set the way,
A love story etched in each step, night or day.

"Melody of Hearts"

Their love, a moonlit sonata in the night's embrace,
Hearts, like instruments, yielding notes of grace,
A love tale resounding for all to perceive,
Played in the moon's gentle, silvery weave.

In their love, each heartbeat a dulcet refrain,
Harmonious rhythms, emotions unchain,
Their connection, a melody to mend and soothe,
Guiding souls in this odyssey, their love's true groove.

Day by day, their love thrives and amplifies,
Instruments of their hearts, cherished as prized,
A duet of passion that through nights takes flight,
Their love's melody, an everlasting light.

In the depths of their love, it remains steadfast,
Spirits entwined, unwavering, unsurpassed,
A love tale composed, forever to shine,
Their love, a divine melody, forever entwined.

"Cascade of Dreams"

In the currents of dreams, their path they trace,
In the river of hope, where love's ripples embrace,
Their hearts, like mariners, sail through the night,
A love tale inscribed in each gleam of light.

With each bend and curve, their love takes hold,
Love's torrent guides them, as dreams unfold,
Their bond endures, destined to outlast,
A river of feelings, a love unsurpassed.

As they follow the drift of dreams' gentle flow,
Their love story deepens, side by side they go,
In the currents of dreams, their voyage takes flight,
An unbroken connection, radiating its light.

Their love, like a cascade through dreams it streams,
In the ebb and flow, their hearts find their dreams,
On the path of hope, they discover their place,
In the river of dreams, love's eternal embrace.

"Beneath the Stars"

Beneath the eternal celestial dome, they sought solace, hearts entwined in a flawless ballet,
Their love story's inception, cradled within night's tender sway,
Under the quilt of the heavens, grace in a shimmering array.

With each twinkle of the cosmic loom, their bond grew profound,
In the universe's silence, mysteries were wound,
Beneath the starry vault, their voyage unfurled,
As constellations whispered sagas to the watching world.

Under the stars, their souls soared on high,
Love's tale etched in astral ink, written in the sky,
Like stars, their love gleamed, radiant and clear,
An indomitable connection, conquering every fear.

Amidst the stellar enchantment, their love found its seal,
In the constellations' opus, their fate was revealed,
Under the stars' enchantment, their love's journey took flight,
On the limitless cosmic canvas, their love shone ever so bright.

"Sculpting Eternity"

In the tapestry of life, they endeavor to bind,
A man and a woman, their destinies entwined.
With each passing challenge, their resolve does grow,
Sculpting a future together, as the currents flow.

Skilled artisans of destiny, they shape with great care,
Molding their dreams, a masterpiece rare.
In the hands of time, their life takes its form,
A resilient sculpture, weathering each storm.

With strokes of perseverance, their journey begins,
A life so enduring, despite its twists and spins.
In the chapter of existence, amidst the daily race,
They sculpt their lives, finding their place.

A sculpture of years, countless moments shared,
A testament to their love, the burdens they've dared.
In life's embrace, they've found their way,
A shared journey deepening, come what may.

"Rainbow of Emotions"

Within the spectrum of emotions, their love takes its flight,
Hearts painted in vivid, luminescent light.
A love tale woven with each shade's tender trace,
In every hue of passion, their bond finds its place.

Love's kaleidoscope, an odyssey unfurled,
A connection deepening, their love for the world.
In the spectrum of emotions, they carve their own way,
Through every challenge, they persist, come what may.

With a vast array of sentiments, so profound,
Their love narrative continues, unwavering and unbound.
In the embrace of the spectrum, their spirits race,
A love story where emotions interlace.

Their love, like a rainbow arching the sky,
A canvas of feelings none can deny.
Upon the palette of hearts, colors beautifully bloom,
A love story dispelling every hint of gloom.

"Harbor of Hope"

In the Harbor of Hope, their beacon does gleam,
Anchored in faith, love's enduring theme.
Their love tale embarks through tempestuous seas,
A resolute bond, unyielding to the breeze.

United they stand against life's turbulent ride,
In Hope's haven, where love won't subside.
Amidst adversities, they choose to remain,
In the Harbor of Hope, love's steadfast domain.

When doubts crash like waves upon the shore,
Hope they clasp onto, forevermore.
In the Harbor of Hope, their love resides,
A guiding light through life's relentless tides.

Their love, an unwavering, radiant lighthouse's beam,
Steering through trials, like a beautiful dream.
In the Harbor of Hope, their spirits take flight,
A love story aglow with undying light.

"Gentle Rain of Affection"

Beneath the gentle rain of affection's sweet embrace,
Two hearts took shelter, love's story they would trace.
Their tale unfurled, drop by tender drop's caress,
Love nurtured beneath the boundless sky's largesse.

With every raindrop that graced the earth's expanse,
Their love deepened, steadfast in its advance.
An unyielding bond, in the face of tempest's wail,
In the rhythm of raindrops, their love set sail.

As raindrops descended, a melody pure and true,
Their hearts entwined, in this love they grew.
Each drop upon their skin, a promise to abide,
A love that flourished, untamed and untied.

In the soft rain's embrace, destiny they'd discern,
A love tale preordained, forever to burn.
Washing away all doubts, like rain on parched ground,
A bond in abundance, forever unbound.

In the soothing touch of raindrops, a love's sweet refrain,
Their love story flourished, complete and humane.
In the tender rain's embrace, they found their delight,
A love that endured, a beacon forever bright.

"Ripples of Joy"

In the waltz of hearts, a joyous serenade,
No tempest can subdue, no hindrance cascade.
Their love story, a canvas of mirthful decree,
A bond fortified with each shared jubilee.

Within laughter's embrace, they discover their way,
A connection burgeoning, with each passing day.
Their spirits ascend in harmonious flight,
A love tale thriving, radiant and bright.

Laughter, akin to waves in the boundless sea,
Crafts ripples of love, wild and carefree.
Their hearts, in cadence and verse, intertwine,
A connection everlasting, a love so divine.

Their love, a ripple touching the very core,
An indomitable bond forevermore.
In the resonance of joy, their love's deployed,
A love story whispered in ripples, enjoyed.

"Horizon's Promise"

They ventured where the horizon's tender kiss did ignite,
Seeking a destiny, a realm of infinite light,
An unseen future, where hearts could orchestrate,
Their love tale, painted with colors so innate.

With each stride into the uncharted's fond embrace,
Their connection deepening, love's luminous grace,
With the assurance of each forthcoming morn, hearts did soar,
A bond resilient, forever to the core.

As the sun bid adieu to yesterdays gone by,
They discovered fresh beginnings, aiming for the sky,
In the promise of horizons yet unfurled,
Their love story, in new splendor, unfurled.

With hearts intertwined, destiny's call embraced,
Hand in hand, their love story's past effaced,
In the boundless promise of horizons far and wide,
Their love deepened, forever side by side.

"Candlelit Whispers"

In the candle's gentle flicker, hearts ignite,
Conversations unfurl in the still of the night,
Words akin to flames, casting a soft glow,
A love tale whispered in the quiet undertow.

With each candle's dance, their bond gains in might,
Love's embrace deepens, in the soft candlelight,
In this intimate hush enveloping the air,
A connection forged, tender and rare.

As candles waltz, secrets take flight,
In the night's silence, their hearts unite,
Confessions in hushed tones, sincere and true,
A love story blossoms, becoming a part of their view.

Words, like candles, guide them through the gray,
Illuminating their path, both night and day,
In candlelit whispers, their story takes its stand,
A bond of pure intimacy, eternal and grand.

"Dance of Fate"

In destiny's domain, two souls took their flight,
Guided by unseen hands, day and night,
A mystical ballet, a dance so profound,
Their steps whispered secrets, hearts tightly wound.

In this dance of destiny, naught to abandon or betray,
They wove shared moments, following destiny's array,
Love's choreography etched in the sands of time,
A dance of two hearts, in a harmonious rhyme.

With each graceful gesture, stories unfurled,
Fate's dance ensnared their world, an enigmatic whirl,
Hearts synchronized, fearless and free,
In the dance of destiny, their love would be.

A rhythm known only to them, in a dance so pure,
Hearts aligned, in each other they'd endure,
Their path uncovered, a love story's sway,
With every rise and fall, they'd find their way.

Two souls in celestial romance, fate's thread they'd tread,
In this dance of destiny, their love widespread,
A future inexorable, they couldn't evade or deny,
A dance of uncertainty, where their love would lie.

"Chapters of Adventure"

In the volume of adventure, their saga unwound,
A journey of revelation in a vast, mystic bound,
Their hearts, like bold voyagers, sought the uncharted lands,
A love narrative inscribed on untrodden sands.

With each step they ventured, their bond did ensue,
Their connection deepening as they explored what's new,
In the chapters of adventure, they scripted their flight,
A love story blossoming in the day's gentle light.

Hand in hand they embarked, treasures in sight,
In the thrilling pages of adventure's might,
Their spirits soared high, caressed by the heights,
A bond fortified by life's exhilarating rites.

Their love tale, countless chapters yet to unfurl,
A journey of hearts, where dreams did twirl,
In the volumes of adventure, they'd eternally roam,
A love story gleaming like stars far from home.

"Canvas of Togetherness"

Upon the canvas of togetherness, their tale unfurled,
Brushstrokes of companionship, from dusk to the world.
A vivid, audacious life they sought to conceive,
A journey of togetherness, their love would cleave.

With every stroke, their connection did swell,
A masterpiece of love, a story to foretell.
Upon the canvas of togetherness, hearts intertwined,
A bond unbreakable, in every crease enshrined.

No distance could force their love to dissever,
As they painted their lives in unity, forever.
Shared dreams and care, the hues they'd employ,
Their love story flourished in strokes of joy.

A canvas of togetherness, a tale laid bare,
A love distinct, a story beyond compare.
Their hearts, side by side, in unity reside,
In the vibrant palette of love, their tale would not hide.

"Eternal Embrace"

In the timeless embrace, two souls entwine,
A love story etched in stars, a celestial design,
Their hearts, like constellations, forever aligned,
A bond unbroken, through the vastness of time.

With each tender touch, their spirits find solace,
A connection deepening, a harmonious embrace,
In the timeless union, their love takes flight,
A sanctuary of hearts, radiant and bright.

As their arms enfold, the universe contained,
In their love's warm glow, all mysteries explained,
In the timeless embrace, they carve their place,
A love story written with enduring grace.

Their love, an embrace beyond finite bounds,
A connection that grows, with each heartbeat's sounds,
In the timeless embrace, their spirits combine,
A love story eternal, forever to shine.

Chapter 3
The Breakup

"Chasing Ghosts"

Pursuing specters of days bygone,
Shadows within the mind's eye drawn,
An endless chase, a relentless quest,
Memories that never offer rest.

Each shadow, a fading tableau,
A glimpse of what once did glow,
No way to reverse time's cruel hand,
Just chasing ghosts across this endless land.

The echoes of laughter, now faint and fleeting,
No solace in memories' ceaseless repeating,
Ghosts of the past, lingering and swaying,
Haunt him every night and day, never decaying.

His history dances just out of grasp,
An apparition, lessons that firmly clasp,
But the past is gone, he can't unwind,
Just chasing ghosts within his innermost mind.

"Distant Constellations"

Our love, a constellation in the distant sky,
Once radiant, now fading, a heartfelt sigh,
No way to bridge the chasm that galaxies divide,
Just distant stars, our love's light faded, hearts cast aside.

Each sparkle once foretold the dreams we'd chase,
Now distant, cold, lost in celestial space,
No hope to fill the vast expanse so stark,
Just distant stars, where love's secrets embark.

Our hearts, once luminous in cosmic embrace,
Now adrift, distant, lost in love's astral race,
No strength to reunite what's drifted astray,
Only distant constellations where our love can't stay.

Our love, once a celestial tale, warmth untold,
Now turned to ice, a story grown cold,
No way to rekindle the warmth of days of yore,
Just distant constellations, our love's lore.

"Lost Compass"

He roams aimlessly through the darkest of nights,
No guiding stars, no glimmer of pale moonlight,
No compass to steer his weary flight,
Just a lost navigator, entangled in his plight.

In an unjust world, each step is heavy with dread,
A stumbling odyssey where despair is widespread,
No salvation in sight, no rescue thread,
Just a lost compass in his heart, heavy as lead.

The needle once steady now spins and swirls,
No longer true, amidst life's ceaseless whirls,
Direction fades as love's tapestry unfurls,
Leaving him adrift, where heartache hurls.

His journey, without a compass, has lost its way,
No path to guide him to a brighter day,
Emotions frozen in the cold, stark dismay,
A love once mighty, now faded and gray,
No compass to lead, as he's led astray.

"Solitary Rain"

Tears cascade like rain, a dolorous refrain,
Each drop narrates a chapter of sorrow's quiet strain.
No ear to heed, no arms to console,
In the tempest of his heart, an untold tale takes its toll.

No love's canopy, no haven from the storm,
Just tears in a heart that's aged and worn.
The rain persists, relentless and strong,
A downpour of anguish, a soul's mournful song.

No end appears, no sun on the morrow,
No rainbow to brighten the world so hollow.
Just solitary tears, in a callous embrace,
In the downpour of life, seeking solace and grace.

His tears, akin to raindrops, whisper despair,
Each one a plea, a wordless prayer.
A cadence all his own, a song to brave,
In the symphony of tears, his spirit to save.

"Fading Echoes"

Love wanes like an echo, distant and faint,
A memory in the shadows, a bittersweet taint,
Just a forgotten echo, where love used to reside,
Each reverberation recalls our love's tender ride.

No hope remains to rekindle what's now lost,
No resurrection of the past, no matter the cost,
Just echoes fading, like whispers in the night,
A memory of love that once burned so bright.

Voices, once teeming with life, now a subdued strain,
No warmth in the waning echoes' domain,
Just distant memories, like a fleeting glance,
In life's cruel landscape, our love had no chance.

Like an echo in the canyon, it fades into the gray,
No chance of revival, no more to convey,
No solace in memories that linger and flow,
Just fading echoes, where love used to glow.

"Silent Goodbyes"

Cold as winter's breath, each blade, sharp and keen,
Deeper than death, a fracture in what had been,
No solace in the stillness, just voids, empty spaces,
Love laid bare, leaving desolation in its traces.

The first, a whisper heard faintly in the night,
A fracture in the silence, love's initial blight,
No warmth in their gaze, just a muted, mournful cry,
Love slowly withers, fading like the sky.

The second, a tremor, a crack in the façade,
A chasm growing wide, love's foundation flawed,
No solace in the silence that lingers in the air,
Just silent farewells, a love beyond repair.

The third, a silence profound, deep, and complete,
A canyon of emptiness, no words can compete,
No tears to shed, no comfort in deceit,
Just silent partings as love's flame does retreat.

The last, a void left in the aftermath,
A vacuum of emotions, love split in half,
No hope in the echoes of their last silent cries,
Just a silent farewell as love, in quiet, finally dies.

"Echoing Silence"

Silence resounds loudly, where once was a symphony,
A void in the air where laughter used to be.
No warmth to enfold, just coldness and despair,
In the lack of voices, love's absence laid bare.

Each moment now lingers, stark and empty,
No love's sweet whispers in the shadows so plenty.
The silence envelops, a suffocating cloak,
In its unyielding grasp, pain cries out and spoke.

Rooms once vibrant with joy now stand forlorn,
No laughter in their halls, no voices to adorn.
Just resounding silence, where emptiness grows,
In their absence, a void, a painful throes.

Their absence, a chasm, a cruel, gaping maw,
No way to fill the void left by their withdraw.
No solace in the echo, no comfort it bears,
Just echoing silence, a weight that despairs.

A constant companion, this silence we bear,
In its cold, lonely embrace, we seek repair.
But within its quiet, we must find our way,
Through echoing silence, into the light of the day.

"Shadows of Love"

In the realm of shadows, they endure,
Love's haunting echoes, steadfast and pure.
Chilling and stark, they navigate the dark,
Ghostly remnants of love, where memories embark.

No warmth in these remnants, only a poignant air,
Shadows of love, where pain's echo is laid bare.
Each shadow a memory, haunting and cold,
The past's grip unyielding, its stories retold.

No light to dispel the lingering gloom,
In the depths of the shadows, love's somber costume.
No escape from love, its presence sincere,
Only shadows of love, where affection appears.

These spectral affections glide, ghostly and near,
No evasion from love, its presence clear.
No hope in the depths where memories stay,
Only shadows of love in love's slow decay.

Their love, like shadows, close and profound,
No erasing the past, no remedy found,
No solace in shadows that endlessly roam,
Just shadows of love that make their heart's home.

"Echoes of Longing"

Echoes of yearning, they linger and persist,
In a haunting chorus, their tales they insist.
A relentless pull, love's hold won't recede,
No end to the echoes, their plea, their need.

Each echo is a cry, from the depths of desire,
No way to quench the yearning's burning fire.
No solace in longings, they never release,
Just an echo of yearning, love's everlasting lease.

Voices of longing, once resounding and bold,
Now spectral murmurs, their fervor growing cold.
There's no hope in echoes that endlessly chime,
Just an echoing yearning, where memories of love climb.

His heart, an echo chamber, repeats love's song,
No escape from emotions, they prove to be strong.
No respite from yearnings that forever remain,
Just an echo of longing, in love's eternal chain.

"Fading Aftershocks"

Fading tremors in life's altered terrain,
A seismic shift in love's disheartening reign,
No respite from the quakes, they persist in their strain,
Just fading tremors, the heart's enduring pain.

A life exposed, each tremor a stark reminiscence,
Of love's decline, torn asunder, once in existence,
No halt to the shaking, no end to the persistence,
Only fading tremors, hearts in a relentless resistance.

The ripples of their love, once tranquil and serene,
Now dissipate like memories, each bond in-between,
No respite from the shuddering, the pain unforeseen,
Just fading tremors in a love's altered scene.

His life, a landscape forever marked and scarred,
No escape from reverberations, emotions unbarred,
No end to the quivering, the heart forever marred,
Fading tremors in love's story, deeply charred.

"Missing Pieces"

Their love, akin to a jigsaw puzzle, once vivid and whole,
Now bereft of pieces, lost in the heart's silent toll,
A tangled tapestry of emotions, shattered, and cold,
No path to repair, no resolution to behold.

Each piece adrift in the abyss of despair,
No promise of reconstruction, a love beyond repair,
Void spaces where affection once breathed a shared air,
In this fractured jigsaw, a story hard to bear.

The picture they once painted, vibrant and complete,
Now splintered, fragments at their feet,
No avenue for restoration, no melodies sweet,
Just an empty disarray where love's echoes fleet.

"Unraveled Threads"

A tapestry, once woven with threads so fine,
Now unravels in the cold of the nighttime,
No hope lingers to mend what's come undone,
Just fraying threads, one by one.

The fabric of love, once robust and profound,
Now lies in tatters, its echoes no longer resound,
But there's no chance to restore what's torn and bare,
Just unraveling threads beyond repair.

Each stitch that once held, now breaks and unwinds,
A bond no longer within its sacred confines,
No strength remains to mend what's torn,
Just unraveling threads, forever forlorn.

Their love, once a masterpiece, now in disarray,
No words to bridge the growing abyss, no way,
No hope to salvage what's left behind,
Only unraveling threads, love's essence declined.

"Torn Love Letters"

Love, a dream shattered, fragments strewn,
A heart in pieces beneath the sorrowful moon,
Torn love letters, once aflame with desire,
Now broken verses, a love lost in mire.

Words of affection, once vivid and bold,
Now torn asunder, a story left untold,
Every letter, every stanza, now scarred,
A love's decline, deeply charred.

Ink that once flowed with fiery grace,
Now a fading memory, a distant trace,
No future to explore, no love to ignite,
Only torn love letters in the night.

Lost in the relentless thunder's roar,
Pages of love's tale exist no more,
Ruins of a once-vibrant rose,
In shattered fragments, their love encloses.

Paper hearts, fractured and worn,
No chance to reconstruct what's forever torn,
In the remnants of their love's remains,
Lie the echoes of heartaches and pains.

"Wilted Roses"

Once in full bloom, their love's vibrant array,
Now withered and faded, in twilight's sway,
Consumed by shadows, no fragrance to bear,
Only the scent of twilight, in love's deep despair.

Love's beauty, once radiant, now fragile and frail,
Each petal a memory, lost in twilight's veil,
No chance to rekindle what once used to gleam,
Wilted roses remain, in love's fading dream.

The thorns that once guarded, no solace to find,
No love's gentle whispers, no passions entwined,
The garden of love, now a desolate land,
Only wilted roses, in love's final stand.

Their love was a garden, once vibrant and grand,
Now lost to the night, no way to withstand,
No dawn on the horizon, no chance to resume,
Just wilted roses, in love's silent gloom.

"Cracked Reflection"

In the mirror, I see a fractured reflection,
A shattered image, a soul's disconnection,
No hope to mend what's fractured inside,
Just fragmented reflections where emotions hide.

Each crack, a symbol of the pain I bear,
No way to repair what the heart cannot spare,
No solace in this fractured glass so cruel,
Just fragmented reflections, a heart's inner duel.

Eyes that once shone, now veiled in sorrow,
No light to guide through the labyrinth tomorrow,
No chance to heal this wound so deep,
Just fragmented reflections, where emotions weep.

My reflection, like my heart, broken and scarred,
No way to rebuild what's eternally marred,
No hope in the pieces that remain,
Just fragmented reflections, concealing the pain.

"Crumbling Castle"

Once a fortress, majestic, firm, and grand,
Now in ruins, surrendering to the land,
No longer standing tall, it crumbles down,
Just falling walls, a silent, mournful crown.

Each stone a memory, aged and scarred,
No way to mend what's now marred,
In the aftermath of love's relentless storm,
Crumbling fortress walls, a fading artform.

The moat once filled with passion's flame,
Now still waters, love's last claim,
No drawbridge left, no passage to seek,
Only crumbling walls, where love grew weak.

Their love, once unyielding, solid, and pure,
Now reduced to debris, a heartache to endure,
No resurrection in the ruins they survey,
Just crumbling fortress walls where love did decay.

"Withered Spring"

Once a spring, brimming with vibrant life's grace,
Now faded, colors vanished without a trace,
The beauty endures, it's but a ghostly reflection,
No blossoms to adorn the once-lush connection.

Each bud, once promising, now fragile and frail,
No hope to revive what love once set sail,
No warmth in the earth's tender embrace,
Just a withered spring, a love's forlorn face.

Once painted in nature's embrace so divine,
Now pale and desolate, love's colors decline,
No hope in the seasons as they drift by,
Just a withering spring, where love's echoes die.

Their love, once a spring, vibrant and bright,
Now withering softly, like the fading twilight,
No way to recapture what's no longer near,
Just a withering spring, where love's end is clear.

"Fading Footprints"

Once bold, now etched in sand, they fade from view,
A presence diminishing, in life's course they undo,
No weight within these footprints as they wane,
Just fading marks in a world forever changed.

Each step, a testament to the march of time's grace,
No halt to the fading, no escape, no embrace,
No solace in the prints left in life's grand scheme,
Just fading footprints, as if life's become a dream.

The world once acutely felt each step he'd take,
Now unaware, as he withdraws, decisions he'll make,
No hope in the tracks that slowly fade away,
Just fading footprints, where life turns to gray.

His presence, akin to these trails in the sand,
No way to halt the fading, as time's shifting hand,
No escape from the encroaching shadows near,
Just fading footprints, as life disappears.

"Forgotten Echoes"

Love fades like an echo, distant, and it's true,
A whisper of the heart, where once we both knew,
Just a fading echo, in the corridors of the past,
Each resonance is a reminder of our love that couldn't last.

There's no hope of rekindling what has slipped away,
No way to resurrect the moments of yesterday,
Just echoes vanishing, like whispers in the breeze,
A memory of love now dancing as a tease.

Voices once alive, now a distant song,
No warmth in these echoes, emotions have gone wrong,
Just distant memories, like a fleeting dream,
In life's complexity, our love lost its gleam.

Like an echo in the mountains, it fades into the night,
No possibility of revival, no path to set right,
No consolation in memories that come and go,
Just forgotten echoes, where love used to flow.

"Empty Melodies"

His life, a once joyful serenade,
Now plays a melancholic masquerade,
Tunes that once soared in a symphony grand,
Now quiet notes in a desolate land.

No melodies to uplift, no harmonies to inspire,
No rhythm for dancing, no reason to aspire,
In this mournful symphony, shadows do abide,
A haunting lament where joy tries to hide.

Endless verses linger, telling tales of woe,
No happiness remains, only echoes of sorrow,
Yet in the depths of this melancholy sea,
A spark of hope may emerge and set him free.

"Lost Constellations"

Love, a constellation lost in the endless night,
Once brilliant, now concealed in obsidian's might,
No guiding stars to repair what's gone amiss,
A love that once soared, now drifting, remiss.

Each star, a memory, hidden from sight,
No way to rekindle love's celestial light,
No hope in the shadows, no guiding star's kiss,
Only a lost constellation, fading into the abyss.

Their love, once vibrant, now a distant gleam,
A night sky once adorned, now a fading dream,
Stars that once radiated, now lost in the scheme,
In the realm of vanishing constellations, love's esteem.

In the expanse of the night, their love has waned,
No beacon to guide, no ember regained,
The constellation of love, forever restrained,
In the vast cosmic canvas, their story remains ingrained.

"Distant Horizon"

The horizon, once a vow, now a great divide,
An emotional abyss, where love couldn't bide,
No bridges span, no pathways left to guide,
Just a distant horizon, where love couldn't confide.

Each mile stretches wide, like a cavernous chasm,
No passage to traverse, in this emotional spasm,
The growing rift, a deep, unforgiving schism,
In that distant horizon, love's vanishing prism.

A bond that's unraveled, once fervent and true,
Now torn asunder, its fire subdued,
In the vastness of the distance, their story is through,
A love like a distant horizon, forever askew.

No chance to reclaim what's now far away,
No teachings in the distance, no emerging day,
The love they once knew, now in disarray,
In that distant horizon, where love had to stray.

"Winds of Isolation"

He stands alone in isolation's biting breeze,
A solitary figure, burdened by life's unease,
No warmth within the chilling winds that tease,
Only isolation's gusts, a heart's unease.

Each wind gust carries whispers of what's lost,
No soothing touch, no matter the cost,
No solace in the chill, a love once embossed,
Just isolation's winds, where emotions exhaust.

The air, once filled with laughter, now cold and vast,
A void where once his heart found steadfast,
His spirit's flag, flying in solitude's blast,
In winds of isolation, his hopes are downcast.

The tempest of his loneliness won't cease,
A relentless force, it offers no release,
In isolation's winds, his heart's inner piece,
A lone soul adrift, seeking love's sweet increase.

"Fading Photographs"

Dimming photographs, memories in shades of gray,
Colors that once danced, now gently decay,
In these frozen frames, moments softly sway,
As dimming photographs bear the weight of the day.

Each snapshot a fragment of days long past,
No alchemy to revive what couldn't last,
In these dimming images, we hold steadfast,
The echoes of history, in memories amassed.

No power to resurrect what time does erase,
As the hues of yesteryears slowly efface,
Faces once vivid, now find their own space,
In dimming photographs, where time we embrace.

Yet even as colors gracefully retreat,
The soul of those moments remains complete,
Dimming photographs may lose their heartbeat,
But the memories they cradle, forever sweet.

"Drowning in Silence"

He drifts in the sea of thoughts, an anchor in his soul,
No escape from the depths where his emotions take their toll.
Each thought a crashing wave, relentless, fierce, and cold,
Tormented by stories, his spirit's tale unfolds.

Sinking in the silence, he struggles to find his way,
No lifeline to cling to, in this darkness, he must stay.
Regrets like shadows haunt him, never letting go,
Just sinking in the silence, where his fears continue to grow.

The silence surrounds him, like water all around,
No surface to break through, no refuge to be found.
In the depths of his own mind, he's trapped in the tide,
Just sinking in the silence, where his thoughts coincide.

His thoughts, like riptides, pull him deeper within,
No way to break their grip, in this watery, endless spin.
His mind is held captive, in this abyss he's confined,
Just sinking in the silence, with thoughts intertwined.

"Fragile Horizon"

The future, a fragile and uncertain dream,
Like a wounded bird, lost in the moon's gleam,
No guarantees of brighter days to find,
Just fragile horizons, where doubts unwind.

Each step they take, a trembling walk,
On paths unknown, in this world's vast talk,
Uncertainty lingers with every stride,
In these fragile horizons, where hope may hide.

Dreams that once filled their hearts with fire,
Now delicate as petals, a fragile desire,
No certainty that they'll rekindle the flame,
In these fragile horizons, love's a tender game.

Their love, once mighty, now a fragile thread,
No way to restore what's now so widely spread,
No strength left to mend what's become frail,
In these fragile horizons, their love's final trail.

The future stretches out, uncertain and unknown,
No map to guide them, no seeds to be sown,
No promises beneath the starry sky,
Just fragile horizons, where love's journey may lie.

"Shattered Reflection"

In the mirror's depths, a fractured soul's lament,
Each shard, a piece of love's intricate descent,
Once complete, now shattered, scarred, and torn,
A heart exposed, in fragments, deeply worn.

No hope resides within this shattered glass,
No gleam through the fractures, as moments pass,
No promises to follow, only what's been lost,
Love's beauty, now reduced to shards, the cost.

His eyes, once radiant, now bear sorrow's weight,
A yearning for redemption, to change love's fate,
Within this shattered glass, a truth laid bare,
A heart in pieces, searching for repair.

No gleam within the gaze, just memories and tears,
Of love's tender moments, now buried in the years,
In fractured mirrors, his reflection speaks,
Of love that's dimmed, like stars, grown weak.

In brokenness, he seeks to find his way,
To mend the mirror, where love's colors sway,
For in the shards, a chance for love to mend,
And heal the heart, on this journey's bend.

"Echoes of Regret"

Regret, an unending echo in the mind's deep well,
A mournful dance, where memories dwell,
No comfort found in thoughts that twist and churn,
Only the ceaseless echo of regret's return.

Each choice, a specter haunting, won't release,
No going back, no way to find peace,
Unanswered questions linger, unresolved,
In the echo of regret, our sorrows are involved.

The past, a canvas painted in hues of rue,
No rewinding time, no change to undo,
Decisions weigh heavy, their shadows persist,
In the echoing chambers where regrets subsist.

Only the vignette of remorse, a shadow's refrain,
A path of sorrow, etched in our life's terrain,
No turning back, no altering fate's directive,
Just the relentless echo of regrets subjective.

Chapter 4
Depression

"Whispers of Darkness"

A choir of murmurs, relentless and severe,
In the chambers of his soul, they linger, clear.
No refuge from the shadows, they taunt and pry,
No respite from their torment, as they multiply.

His conscience, an unwavering judge, declares its stand,
In the corners of his mind, it never loosens its hand.
No sanctuary in silence, no peace in which to hide,
No escape from the relentless voices deep inside.

His thoughts, once gentle whispers, now like a tempest's roar,
A storm of inner battles, a mind's internal war.
The voices, once soothing, have grown stern and cold,
There's no escaping this inner turmoil, as the story unfolds.

No consolation in this ceaseless, inner strife,
In the maze of his mind, he wrestles with life.
No liberation from a mind that seems too frail,
Yet in this relentless struggle, he searches for a brighter trail.

"Silent Storms"

Beneath a placid surface, tempests lay in wait,
Unspoken emotions, a storm's uncertain state.
A whirlwind of feelings, his heart does confuse,
Unvoiced thoughts in a turbulent ruse.

Each tempest a turmoil, words left unsung,
Inner chaos abounds, a maelstrom unsprung.
No lightning to illuminate his inner strife,
Just silent storms, concealed deep in life.

Calm as the surface, a façade of serenity,
Yet turmoil below, where emotions find infinity.
No trace of the battles his soul does endure,
Just silent storms, where his heart's tumult is obscure.

Hidden and profound, like tempests that reside,
Emotions churn, no sign of respite beside.
No comfort in the stillness that pretends,
Just silent storms, where his spirit transcends.

"Drowning In Darkness"

Engulfed in shadows, gasping for air,
In the abyss of despair, a relentless affair.
No glimmer of hope, just darkness to bear,
Just drowning in shadows, in this heavy snare.

Lost in a world where light can't intrude,
Each breath is a struggle, a battle pursued.
No escape from the shroud that tightly grips,
Only drowning in shadows, as hope slowly slips.

Once illuminated by stars up above,
Now a void so profound, devoid of their love.
No dawn on the horizon, no flicker of light,
Just drowning in shadows, a perpetual fight.

His life adrift, lost in an endless sea,
No guiding star, no chance to break free.
In the depths of the abyss, he's tragically bound,
Drowning in shadows, where despair is unbound.

"Rain of Sorrows"

Tears fall like rain, a heavy, unyielding tide,
A tempest of emotions, nowhere to hide,
Storm clouds gather, dark and full of despair,
Each drop is a testament to the weight he bears.

No shelter from this downpour, this torrential rain,
No end in sight, only anguish and pain,
In the relentless deluge of sorrow's might,
Each tear, a drop of darkness, in the heart of the night.

The once-clear sky, now obscured by grief's veil,
No respite from the tears, as they relentlessly assail,
No hope in the horizon, no relief from the strain,
Just an endless cascade of sorrows, a heart's heavy chain.

His tears, like raindrops, fall in a ceaseless stream,
No way to escape the turmoil, no hope, no gleam,
In this unending storm of sorrow, he's caught,
A torrential downpour of emotions, an ocean of thought.

"Echoes of Lost Joy"

The echoes of joy, distant and faint,
In the vast tapestry of life's painted paint,
A melody that once filled the soul's wide dome,
Now distant, a memory of love's sweet home.

No solace in the whispers of days of yore,
Just echoes of moments that are no more,
The resonance of joy, a gentle breeze,
In the chambers of the heart, where love did ease.

Ghosts of laughter in the misty air,
Recalling moments when love was everywhere,
Yet, there's no turning back life's ceaseless climb,
Only echoes of lost joy, marking the time.

His heart, an echoing chamber, it holds,
A constant refrain, where memories unfold,
No way to rewind the hands of time's own clock,
Just echoes of lost joy, in life's winding walk.

In the echoes, love's memories reside,
A bittersweet reminder of the love that once had tied,
No solace in the fading, distant sound,
Only echoes of lost joy in the heart are found.

"Broken Reflection"

In the mirror's gaze, a fractured truth,
A shattered soul, worn down, uncouth,
No solace in the broken pieces there,
No respite from the world's heavy despair.

The fragments tell stories of a life well worn,
But hold no answers to the sorrows borne,
No warmth resides within these fractured bits,
No way to change life's complex, winding scripts.

Once vibrant eyes, now weathered by years,
No chance to dispel the world's silent fears,
As the reflection fades, so does the gleam,
In a world where hope feels like a fading dream.

His image, a reflection of life's grand quest,
A journey, scarred and well-addressed,
Yet in those fractured shards, resilience lies,
A spirit enduring, despite life's endless ties.

"Ink of Sorrow"

Tears, like ink, in somber shades,
Stain the parchment where his heart cascades.
A somber palette, where once love was sketched,
Now, ink of sorrow, where emotions are etched.

Each tear drop tells a story of despair,
No erasing, no escape from the tearful affair.
No ink to rewrite the pages of his heart,
Just ink of sorrow, where pain plays its part.

The well of joy has run dry and still,
In the silent chamber where his sorrows distill.
No hopeful quill, no brighter ink to choose,
Just ink of sorrow, as emotions refuse to lose.

His tears, like ink, mark the passage of time,
Staining the verses of life's intricate rhyme.
No whiteness to blot out what has been,
Just ink of sorrow, a tale of loss and sin.

Yet within the ink, resilience does reside,
A testament to the strength he can't hide.
In the strokes of sorrow, his heart's grace,
A portrait of a soul that still finds its place.

"Shadowed Horizon"

The horizon cloaked in shadows, the future veiled in the night,
A labyrinth of obscurity, no gleam of hopeful light.
Uncertain, it lingers, the enigma yet untold,
No solace in this darkness, no future in its hold.

In life, colors once vivid fade to muted grays,
The once-clear path obscured by a shadowy haze.
Unfathomable destinies concealed within the night,
No hope within these shadows, where dreams take their flight.

His journey echoes through the shrouded, watchful skies,
A path concealed, where no sun truly lies.
No revelation beckons, no promise in disguise,
Just the shadowed horizon, where hope never dies.

"Hollow Melodies"

Hollow melodies whisper in a world askew,
Notes bereft of vitality, lost in the evening dew.
Life's rhythm stripped away, adrift at sea,
Each note a ghostly echo of what used to be.

No path to reclaim what the tides have swept,
No solace in these melodies, mournfully kept.
Hollow tunes linger in the heart's empty space,
The music once vibrant now a mournful trace.

Joy, once woven into each harmonious line,
Now seems distant, a memory in decline.
A symphony persists, carrying on and on,
Hollow melodies persist, as hope seems gone.

His life, once a composition rich and grand,
Now echoes with hollowness across the land.
A mournful tune, a somber refrain prevails,
In these hollow melodies, where meaning often fails.

"Echoes of Longing"

Echoes of longing, they linger and reside,
In a haunting refrain, their stories coincide.
A relentless pull, love's grasp refuses to sway,
No end to the whispers, their plea, their disarray.

Each echo's a cry, from the depths they arise,
No way to silence the yearning in their ties.
No solace in the desires that never release,
Just an echo of longing, a love that won't cease.

Voices of passion, once fervent and clear,
Now spectral whispers, they slowly disappear.
There's no hope in echoes that endlessly sing,
Just an echoing longing, where memories cling.

His heart, an echo chamber, repeats love's lament,
No respite from emotions, no argument.
No escape from the yearning that endlessly springs,
Just an echo of longing, where love forever clings.

"Fading Colors"

Colors have waned, the world's vibrant scene,
The soul now mired in this dim, gray sheen.
No vibrant hues remain to light the way,
Just fading colors in the dim of the day.

Each shade once spoke of moments so bright,
Now memories that fade in the dwindling light.
No solace in this world, so cold and stark,
Just fading colors where hope leaves a mark.

His life's canvas, once vivid, full of thrill,
Now cloaked in gray, an emptiness to instill.
No hope to rekindle what was once so adored,
Just fading colors, love's beauty ignored.

The world, in this spectrum, drained of its zest,
No way to reclaim what has gone to rest.
No comfort can be found in this fading view,
Just fading colors in a world he once knew.

"Cracks in the Mask"

Beneath the mask, where cracks emerge,
A façade of strength, but the soul's own surge.
No strength left to mend, what's now revealed,
Just cracks in the mask, where truths are unsealed.

Each fissure's a chasm, in the mask's façade,
No more concealing the depths they parade.
No comfort in the mask as it slowly declines,
Only cracks in the façade as reality entwines.

The smile that once masked a turbulent sea,
Now splinters and shatters, set emotions free.
No hope to sustain it, as it breaks and slips,
Only the cracks in the mask, where authenticity skips.

This mask, once protection, now crumbles away,
No way to repair it, doubts have their say.
No escape from the cracks that continue to grow,
Only the cracks in the mask, where true feelings flow.

"Veiled Sun"

Happiness, a sun behind the clouded sky,
Struggles, yearning for its chance to shine so high,
No brightness in the shadows that persist,
It's just a veiled sun where joy's light can't exist.

Each ray, once vibrant, now filtered and faint,
No way to break free from this endless restraint,
No solace in the darkness, its relentless toll,
Only a veiled sun, where despair takes control.

The warmth it once shared, now shrouded from view,
No hope to pierce through, no path to renew,
No comfort in the shroud that dims its blaze,
Only a veiled sun, as joy retreats in a daze.

His happiness, that sun, concealed from the sight,
Yearning to break free, to regain its full might,
No glimpse of the radiance that could yet be,
Just a disguised sun, where hope longs to see.

"Sinking Anchor"

He stands in shadows, burdened by despair's weight,
In a realm of endless nights, it's never too late.
No escape from the chains, heavy and tight,
Just a sinking anchor, gripping the night.

Each link's a shackle, a relentless hold,
No comfort in the dark, where his story's been told.
Only a sinking anchor in life's empty swells,
Where solitude dwells and hope often dispels.

The ship, once swift, now anchored in place,
No way to break free from this cold embrace.
No hope in an anchor refusing to rise,
Just a sinking anchorage where dreams meet their demise.

His life's a vessel adrift on the sea,
Sinking in waves of despair, oh, woe is he.
No escape from the depths where dreams are confined,
In this sinking anchorage, hope is enshrined.

"Desolate Canvas"

Life, a blank canvas stretched wide and bare,
No color, no care, no palette to prepare,
No hope upon this empty frame does rest,
Just a life that's lost, a silent, vast emptiness.

Each stroke of memory, a fleeting trace,
Of the beauty once known, of a life's embrace,
No way to resurrect what time has claimed,
No solace in the void, where hope is maimed.

The artistry of his life, once bold and grand,
Now reduced to nothing on this barren strand,
No hope to rekindle the hues that have fled,
Only a desolate canvas, where dreams lie dead.

His world, a blank canvas, cold and gray,
No vibrant shades to brighten his day,
No way to reclaim what's been erased,
Just a barren canvas in sorrow's embrace.

"Lost in Fog"

Amidst a fog of despair, he finds himself astray,
Days veiled in shadow, a chilling disarray.
A mist descends, shrouding sight and sense,
Enveloping thoughts in nocturnal suspense.

Each notion a skirmish against the ethereal haze,
No escape, no respite, caught in its daze.
No solace in the veils that his soul enshroud,
In this relentless fog, emptiness is endowed.

Once luminous and clear, his thoughts now perplex,
In this muddled fog, they twist and interconnect.
No hope as the mist clings tenaciously on,
A mental labyrinth where clarity is gone.

His mind, a landscape forever concealed,
In the fog's embrace, his thoughts are sealed.
No means to break free from its cold grasp,
Just an unending pursuit, an enduring mental clasp.

"Silent Desperation"

In the stillness of despair, a frigid fire's embrace,
A tempest deep within, a veiled and tortured place,
No flight from flames that slowly sear the core,
Only silent anguish, an agony held close evermore.

Every moment a skirmish, a hushed war concealed,
No words can fathom the torment's ceaseless yield,
No solace in the mute bonds that tightly grasp,
Only silent despair, where shadows long last.

Once fervent cries, now stilled and ensnared,
No glimpse of light to break what's scared,
No solace in the hush that swallows his speech,
Only silent desperation, where despair he does beseech.

His heart, a battlefield in ceaseless strife,
No refuge from life's chaotic, ceaseless life,
No respite from the pain that will not depart,
Only silent despair, consuming his heart.

"Whispers of Defeat"

The voices of surrender, an unyielding parade,
A tormenting legion, in shadows they cascade,
Their jeers, like bitter echoes, in a world of tears,
Each murmur is a testament to unfulfilled years.

No escape from the struggles that persist and stay,
No refuge in the echoes of the relentless replay,
Just a murmur of surrender, where hope fades away,
The voices that once cheered now lead him astray.

His spirit, a fortress besieged day by day,
No avenue to shatter the cyclical dismay,
No consolation in the whispers that gnaw and bore,
Just a narrative of surrender, where despair takes more.

His aspirations, once luminous, now seem defiled,
In the face of those voices, like an endless trial,
No path to rekindle the vigor that once shone bright,
Just a murmur of surrender in the battleground of his fight.

"Unspoken Agony"

In the abyss of his soul, a hushed lament,
Unvoiced suffering, where feelings ferment,
Concealed from the world, a profound woe,
A torment that in his heart continues to grow.

No words can grasp the ache he sustains,
Just unspoken suffering, where his inner pains,
A battle waged in quiet, graceful strain,
Away from the world's clamor, its endless chain.

The world remains unaware of his inner fray,
The pain he carries, silent yet heavy to sway,
Wounds that persist, scars that endure,
In the silence, his struggles remain obscure.

Unuttered agony, a life etched with marks,
His pain, a shadow beneath the celestial sparks,
A companion he carries through day and night,
No escape from the ache, from the silent fight.

Yet, amidst this silent despair's domain,
He finds strength in the burdens, the strain,
For deep within the folds of his muted strife,
Resides a resilience that shapes his life.

.

"Broken Compass"

In quivering hands, a fragile compass held,
No guiding needle, just a tale unveiled,
No north to pursue, no journey to embark,
Only a broken compass, tearing through his heart.

Each twist, a gamble, in this wild expanse of woe,
No remedy for what time has cast below,
No solace in knowing he's lost his way,
Just a broken compass that led him astray.

This trusted guide, now fractured, worn, and meek,
No hope to mend it, no language left to speak,
No comfort in the realization of being misplaced,
Only a broken compass, in despair embraced.

A relic of direction, once unwavering and right,
Now shattered and useless in the vastness of the night,
No way to rediscover his course, his past,
No sanctuary from the fear that grips him so fast,
Only a broken compass, as hope fades away,
In the wilderness of existence, where shadows hold sway.

"Solitary Rainclouds"

Lonesome rain clouds wept in the lofty skies,
Carrying burdens, attuned to soul's cries.
No respite from the weight they bore,
Just relentless rain, an endless pour.

Each drop, a tear in the heart's vast well,
Falling in solitude, an echoing knell.
No sanctuary from the downpour's caress,
Only the rain, in its mournful progress.

Mournful rain clouds, where despair takes root,
Once refuge, now veiled, heavy and mute.
No avenue to lift their burdens aloft,
Just the ceaseless rain, a continuous soft.

His solitude akin to clouds that remain,
No escape from the weight, a relentless chain.
Shadows encroach, tireless and near,
Only the rain, echoing his deepest fear.

"Fading Starlight"

Dimming starlight, hope's dwindling ember,
In the night's gentle cradle, it begins to surrender.
Once a radiant guide, now gently it wanes,
No constellations linger, just ephemeral remains.

Each glimmer, a memory of brilliance unfurled,
Fading swiftly, like tales of an ancient world.
No solace in the dimming celestial expanse,
Only fading starlight as moments advance.

The night, erstwhile aglow with dreams profound,
Now an abyss where hope cannot be found.
No more wishes on a falling star's descent,
Just fading starlight in the firmament.

His hope, like fading starlight, slips from his grasp,
No clasp can retain it, no prayer to clasp.
No comfort found in the deepening abyss,
Only fading starlight, a vanishing kiss.

"Eclipse of Hope"

Hope, a sun that once blazed in the boundless sky,
Now dimmed by shadows, its fervor awry,
No radiance to pierce the deepening night's sprawl,
Just an eclipse of hope, where despair begins to enthrall.

Each moment's a skirmish to wrest from the dark's embrace,
Suffocating shadows, a relentless interlace,
No respite discovered in the shroud's encompassing sway,
Just an eclipse of hope, where dreams slowly decay.

The light, once so brilliant, now veiled and concealed,
No hope to disperse the shadows, their grip unrevealed,
No hope in the obscurity, its incessant foray,
Just the eclipse of hope in a world turned gray.

His optimism, akin to the hidden sun's gentle gleam,
Concealed from our view, a vanishing dream,
No means to rekindle what the night has entwined,
No release from the darkness that persists undefined.

Yet, an eclipse of hope may yield to dawn's art,
In a world yearning for the caress of hope's start,
For even in obscurity, faint embers may stay,
To rekindle new hope and illuminate the day.

"Shattered Visions"

His dreams, like shattered glass, lie at his feet,
Reflecting fragments of hope, a journey incomplete,
No gleam within these shards that pierce his soul's keep,
Just shattered visions where despair's secrets creep.

Each shard, a fragment of what might have been,
No path to mend what the heart can't win,
No solace in these fragments that shimmer in the gloom,
Just shattered visions, where dreams meet their tomb.

Once dreams sparkled, now broken and still,
No hope to mend what time cannot fulfill,
No mirror of aspirations, unscathed by the past,
Only shattered visions in a world that won't last.

His ambitions, akin to fragile glass, forever fractured,
No means to restore them, no words to be captured,
No solace in the gleaming shards that endure,
Just shattered visions in life's relentless allure.

"Fading Footprints"

Once bold, now etched in sand, they softly recede,
A presence slipping through life's grasp, indeed,
No weight within these footprints as they gently wane,
Just vanishing marks in a world forever changed.

Each step, a testimony to the relentless march of time,
No pause in the fading, no reason, no rhyme,
No solace in the imprints left in life's stead,
Just fading footprints as if memory's thread.

The world once keenly sensed his every stride,
Now unaware, as he withdraws, tries to hide,
No hope in the trails that slowly dissipate,
Just fading footprints, where colors turn to slate.

His presence, much like these fading trails,
No means to stall the retreat, as the world prevails,
No escape from the encroaching shadow's blade,
Just fading footprints, where existence starts to fade.

"Fractured Smile"

His smile, like shards of glass, so finely spun,
A fragile façade, his battles kept undone.
No joy in fragments harboring hidden strife,
No solace in the splinters that mark a wounded life.

In the realm of shadows, his smile dances light,
Once radiant, now brittle, a victim of the night.
No way to mend what the soul keeps sealed away,
No means to restore the masks that fray.

Each shard reflects the echoes of his inner ache,
Mirrors to the wounds he's hesitant to forsake.
Scattered pieces, lost in an endless, starless sky,
A fractured smile concealing the heart's silent cry.

Yet behind this visage, the eyes reveal the truth,
In their depths, the remnants of long-lost youth.
A silent plea for empathy, for some sweet grace,
Still, the fractured smile lingers upon his face.

Within this brokenness, a resilience resides,
A testament to how the human heart abides.
He carries on despite the fractured veneer,
A testament to the strength that perseveres.

The world may glimpse a smile that's cracked and frail,
But beneath it lies a spirit that won't derail.
Amidst the pain and shadows, he stands tall,
A symbol of the fortitude found in us all.

"Eclipsed Horizon"

In the depths of darkness, no glimmer shines bright,
No solace in sight, just the all-encompassing night.
An eclipse on the horizon, a world cast in shade,
A shadowed soul's waltz, a mournful serenade.

No refuge from the veil that stifles our view,
Only an eclipse on the horizon, where dreams bid adieu.
Once radiant vistas now swathed in cold gray,
No path to reclaim what's been taken away.

The shadow keeps growing, its hold unrelenting,
No futures unfolding, no hopes reinventing.
The horizon, once vibrant, now sealed and enclosed,
No dawn breaking through where the dark interposed.

Just an eclipse on the horizon, where hope softly wanes,
In the heart of this darkness, where dreams bear their chains.
Yet still, in the silence, a flicker remains,
A whispered resilience, in spite of the reins.

"Empty Echoes"

The hollow echoes, a lamenting refrain,
Through his very being, they persist, causing pain.
In caverns of void, chaos unfolds its scroll,
No respite in sight as despair claims his soul.

Each echo's a marker of what once was here,
An absence profound, a battle severe.
No way to bridge this chasm so vast,
Just empty echoes, memories amassed.

In chambers once warmed by love's tender grace,
Now echoes endure, carving out a vacant space.
Phantoms of yesteryears, they stubbornly remain,
In this relentless heartache, they cling to their domain.

His heart, an echo chamber, amplifies the cries,
No escape from the haunting, unyielding ties.
No solace from the emptiness, ceaseless it flows,
Just empty echoes where love's torment bestows.

Chapter 5
Healing and Hope

"Whispers of Hope"

In the abyss of despair, where solace is lost,
Amidst shadows deep, at what dreadful cost?
The darkness prevails, its dominion imposed,
Yet in its cold clutch, a faint murmur composed.

A murmur so fragile, a gleam, a faint glow,
In the heart of the void, where our secrets bestow.
Like a lighthouse it shines, through the depths of despair,
A whisper of hope, saying, "Life is still there."

In the shroud of our dread, where the night tightly clings,
There's a glimmer of hope, where a new day begins.
Gentle voices like stars, in the darkness they gleam,
Guiding our hearts towards the first morning beam.

Once distant, now near, as we leave the past behind,
No longer confined by the shackles that bind.
Unraveling shadows that haunt and dismay,
Rebuilding our spirits, as worries decay.

With each tender whisper, a promise unfurls,
A future awaits, with its treasures and pearls.
The ballads of courage, a hopeful refrain,
The future, though uncertain, brings joy and no pain.

So, with every murmur, let's dare to believe,
It's more than a dream; it's a pledge we receive.
A tapestry woven with threads spun from grace,
A future we craft with each whisper's embrace.

"Emerge from Shadows"

From the abyss, the morning's gleam does arise,
A beacon of hope, a new day's surprise.
Escaping the night's clasp, where shadows retreat,
Emerges the radiant light, our terrors unseat.

Each step he now takes exudes strength and pure grace,
With no turning backward, he claims his own space.
No solace in darkness, he greets dawn's embrace,
The pain that once bound him starts fading apace.

Upon the path where dreams had long been deferred,
The burdens of yesteryears softly are stirred.
The weight of the past, now lifted and shed,
His spirit takes flight as new horizons spread.

No longer ensnared by despair's cold embrace,
His life shines anew, past's chains he'll efface.
From shadows emerging, embracing the scope,
Out of the abyss springs forth a fresh hope.

In the depths of the dark where the night seems to reign,
There's strength everlasting to break every chain.
Emerging triumphant, his spirit takes flight,
Unveiling the inner light, banishing the night.

"Echoes of Strength"

Amidst echoes of strength, he carves his own way,
Resonant courage that knows not night nor day.
No weakness or doubt in this steadfast sight,
Within echoes of strength, he finds his guiding light.

Each echo resounds with resilience's decree,
A testament to strength, unforeseen and free.
No longer comforted by shadows' embrace,
Within echoes of strength, he discovers his place.

The voices once silenced, now sing and resound,
A chorus proclaiming he's no longer bound.
No more burdens to tether his soul's gentle grace,
In these echoing fortitudes, he finds his embrace.

His journey unfolds, echoing sounds pave the road,
An angel's whisper guides, a path brightly glowed.
In these resonant strengths, he'll securely case,
Past trials and tribulations leave but a trace.

For within these echoing reverberations, he'll regain,
The spirit and might to endure any pain.
Through life's trials and tribulations, he'll rise to attain,
In the echoes of strength, he'll flourish again.

"Rekindled Flame"

A once feeble flame, now blazing with might,
No more remnants of despair in its light.
In this newfound fire, his story takes flight,
Each spark a promise, a truth shining bright.

No longer ensnared by the shadows of yore,
In this rekindled blaze, his spirit does soar.
The flickering ember, now roaring with grace,
Ignites his fervor, sets dreams in their place.

No more shadows to shroud his inner faith,
In this new-born fire, he conquers the wraith.
His life, like a candle once near despair,
Now ablaze with purpose, beyond compare.

Even in the darkest abyss of his past,
He unearths a flame, steadfast and vast.

"Blossom of Resilience"

In despair's abyss, where shadows do creep,
A courage's bud awakens from sleep,
Through sorrow's dark cracks, it dauntlessly springs,
Strength unfurling as the heart joyously sings.

Petals like armor, with resilience imbued,
In untold tales, their beauty pursued,
Roots delve deep, find strength in the strife,
A bloom of resilience, embracing life.

Though storms may have raged and fierce winds have blown,
This bloom stands unbroken, majestic, alone,
For it knows in its scars, true grace takes its place,
A testament to courage in this solemn space.

A bloom of resilience, its wounds on full view,
Each petal's a triumph, each bloom forged anew,
A tribute to the power of concealed light,
In the darkness, its beauty forever takes flight.

In despair's abyss, it rises above,
A bloom of defiance, a symbol of love,
From pain's very cracks, it soars evermore,
This bloom of resilience, its spirit to adore.

"Mosaic of Recovery"

In fragments, his soul, like shards of glass, did lie,
A mosaic of sorrow beneath a somber sky.
Yet, piece by piece, he sought the strength to mend,
To find healing within, to let his heart transcend.

Each shard, a memory, a lesson, and a scar,
A glimpse into the depths of who and where we are.
No solace in the fragments of days long gone,
But a mosaic of healing, a journey to dawn.

The colors, once dulled, now began to gleam,
As piece by piece, they wove into a dream.
No more chaos reigning, no enduring strife,
In this mosaic of healing, he'd reclaim his life.

With each tender placement, a story did unfold,
A tale of resilience, a spirit strong and bold.
No more grief to burden, no more mourning vast,
His spirit would rediscover itself at last.

A work of art emerging, sturdy and refined,
In this mosaic, his essence was aligned.
For even in fragments, beauty could revive,
In this mosaic of recovery, he'd genuinely come alive.

"Healing Waters"

In waters tranquil, he charts his own way,
Whispers of healing in the soul's grand display.
No tempests of yore, just a gentle, calm flow,
In these waters, his spirit begins to aglow.

Each ripple, a caress, each murmur, pure grace,
He finds his heart's haven, a timeless embrace.
No solace in the tumult of days long since passed,
In these healing waters, a serenity amassed.

The currents once fierce, now tenderly entwine,
Embracing his spirit, a peaceful design.
No more battles to wage, no more weary strife,
In these healing waters, he reclaims his life.

Strolling the stream, a profound peace unfolds,
In the gentle waters, his essence beholds.
No burdens of yesteryears, no shadows cast,
In healing waters, he finds peace at last.

A deep liberation, renewal's sweet cue,
Inner peace within waters, life is made new.
This sanctuary of healing, his soul's sweet refrain,
In tranquility, it shall forever remain.

"Sunrise of Renewal"

In the tranquil hush of dawn's embrace,
The sunrise paints hope, a triumph's trace.
No longer do shadows grasp his might,
In this dawn of renewal, he takes his flight.

Each ray a promise, a fresh genesis,
A testament to strength, his essence's compass.
No more nocturnal doubts, once so ensnared,
In the sunrise of renewal, his spirit was repaired.

A world once veiled in a shroud of despair,
Now bathes him in light, so gentle and rare.
No more haunting doubts that shadowed his days,
In this sunrise of renewal, he charts new pathways.

His life, akin to the day, begins to unfold,
In this dawn of renewal, his tale is retold.
For even in the darkest hours he had wept,
In the sunrise of renewal, he stands redeemed and adept.

"Rebirth of Dreams"

Like the first rays of dawn, hope is born anew,
Filling his heart with dreams, vibrant and true.
No more shadows to obscure his hopeful sight,
In this rebirth of dreams, he welcomes the light.

Each dream, a promise of fires yet to ignite,
No more darkness to cloak his soul's upward flight.
In this rebirth of dreams, his spirit takes wing,
The future, once distant, is now within his spring.

A world of possibilities, free from doubt and dread,
No more burdens to tether, no chains to spread.
This rebirth of dreams sows a seed, a treasure,
His life is a vivid canvas, enduring with pleasure.

Even in the deepest of nights, once so profound,
This rebirth of dreams, his hopes will unbound.
For in the dawn of dreams, he'll firmly cope,
And find in his heart his eternal, enduring hope.

"Harbor of Renewal"

In the tranquil harbor of self-embrace, he's sought,
Renewal whispers like the sea's gentle thought.
Where self-doubt's tempests have faded and ceased,
A new voyage begins, his heart now released.

Each wave a reminder of inner grace's hold,
A testament to the journey, a story unfolds.
No more solace in self-judgment's embrace,
Casting off doubt's waters, he finds his own place.

Shores once distant now beckon with love's allure,
A haven of self-acceptance, enduring and pure.
No more striving to fit another's mold,
In the harbor of renewal, his tale is retold.

Like a ship on the sea, a safe berth he's found,
Truly free, with self-love all around.
Even in life's storms and with challenges to cope,
He's found his eternal, enduring hope.

"Radiant Mornings"

Mornings once veiled in darkness and despair,
Now burst forth, radiant, dispelling all care.
A brand new day rises, brilliantly bright,
No more shadows to quell his inner light.

Each sunrise, a promise, a fresh start unveiled,
Optimism blossoms, like morning's dew hailed.
No more lingering shadows, no sorrow's blight,
In these hopeful mornings, his spirit takes flight.

Where once there was moping, he now finds his way,
The concealed sun reveals its grand display.
Doubts that once clouded his heart and his thought,
Have been vanquished by hope the morning has brought.

With each brightening day, his life soars above,
In this morning's embrace, he rediscovers love.
Even in the depths of night's shadowed cope,
He clings to hope, a steadfast, unbroken rope.

"Sky of Possibilities"

In the boundless sky of dreams, where hopes alight,
There are no shackles to hold him in this endless height.
Each cloud, an opportunity, a chance to ascend,
A canvas of potential where aspirations blend.

No solace in the shadows of yesterday's plight,
In this sky of possibilities, he finds his flight.
The once distant horizon now beckons him near,
A realm of boundless prospects, free from fear.

No longer burdened by the chains of the past,
His spirit soars like a bird, unrestrained at last.
His future expands, like the sky's endless dance,
In this realm of possibilities, he takes his stance.

Even in the darkest of nights where he once did roam,
He's found his true place, an abode and a home.

"Crescendo of Life"

Each note, each chapter, each trial, each song,
Is a memoir of the journey, both brief and long.
But in every refrain, a key does appear,
To build towards a climax, to unshackle and steer.

Life's symphony commences with a gentle refrain,
Innocent notes, free from sorrow or stain.
As the melody evolves, it finds its own way,
Building to a climax, with joy as its ray.

When the music crescendos with grace so divine,
In this zenith of life, you brightly shine.
No longer the doubts that once had their say,
In this zenith of life, your heart leads the way.

Like a grand symphony reaching its crest,
You stand resolute, in the limelight's sweet quest.
Even in the quietest moments where doubts used to cope,
In this zenith of life, you discover endless hope.

"Wings Unfolding"

Like wings unfurling, stretching vast and bold,
His soul yearns to soar, its tale yet untold.
No more bonds of yesteryears, gripping tight,
With wings unfurling, he'll ascend to great height.

Each feather, a lesson, challenge, or grace,
Signs of a journey as he finds his place.
No more solace in the well-worn, the old ways,
With wings unfurling, his spirit now ablaze.

The sky, once too far, now calls him near,
A world of hope, devoid of doubt and fear.
No more burdens to tether, to weigh him down,
With wings unfurling, freedom becomes his crown.

His life, akin to a bird in the splendid light,
With wings extending, he welcomes the flight.
Even in the depths where darkness would grope,
With wings unfurling, he discovers endless hope.

"Resonating Hues"

His emotions waltz in vivid, vibrant hues,
A kaleidoscope of healing, a canvas to infuse,
No longer bound to sorrow's monochrome,
In these resplendent colors, he'll find his own.

Each shade, a feeling, a memory's sweet grace,
A symphony of colors, his heart's warm embrace,
Where he discovers his voice and his song,
No solace in the shadows where he did belong.

Gone are the shades of somber despair,
Life's radiant palette fills the open air,
What was once shrouded now bursts into light,
In these resounding colors, he'll conquer the night.

No more a world cloaked in dreary gray,
These colors guide him along his way,
His heart, a canvas, now alive and bright,
In these resounding colors, he'll take flight.

A story unfolds with each brush, each stroke,
Even in the darkest times, hope awoke,
Where once he was lost in life's subdued cues,
He'll find his colorful muse, his path to choose.

"Canvas of Tomorrow"

The canvas of tomorrow, pristine and vast,
Holds boundless promise, a chance to recast.
The brushstrokes of yesteryears begin to wane,
On this canvas of tomorrow, a fresh terrain.

Each stroke, each choice, each dream's ascent,
Weaves a tale of resilience, a testament.
No more solace in the past's dwindling view,
He paints his own narrative, strong and true.

Once-muted colors now vividly ignite,
The story unfolds, bathed in newfound light.
No longer confined by the past's worn lines,
His spirit soars free as hope intertwines.

His life's an empty canvas, awaiting the hand,
On this canvas of tomorrow, he takes a stand.
Even in the darkest hours, where he once plod,
Hope springs eternal in a canvas awed.

"Wings of Hope"

From darkness to light, the journey unrolls,
Despair's metamorphosis, where hope now consoles.
The burdens, once crushing, become our might,
As darkness withdraws, we follow the light's flight.

In the realm of despair, a faint spark appears,
Where gravity's pull finds wings through our tears.
The old sighs surrender to breath anew,
As gravity yields to growth, life blooms and renews.

The ties that restrained us now break apart,
Sorrow's retreat, replaced by a hopeful heart.
Where darkness once held sway, now shines the light,
From despair to hope, our spirits take flight.

"Echoes of Gratitude"

In quiet moments, when the world takes repose,
He hears the reverberation of gratitude, deeply composed.
No more bitterness, anger, or weary strife,
Gone are the fears and sorrows, for once in his life.

No longer burdened by the pain of days gone by,
In these echoes of gratitude, he finds peace nearby.
Each whisper is a testament to growth and grace,
No more dwelling on loss or anguish to embrace.

No regrets for the past, no more sorrows to bear,
Just joy in the present, and a future laid bare.
Memories once weighty now carry a gentle trace,
He's found his place; his heart finds its space.

No more mourning the past's somber view,
In the echoes of gratitude, his spirit anew.
Even in the darkest hours, where he used to mope,
He discovers boundless gratitude in the echoes of hope.

"Blossom of Joy"

Joy, a flower that unfurls in the sun's warm embrace,
Nurtured by healing, it finds its destined place.
The journey unfurls, and darkness is undone,
His spirit radiates, resolute, like the morning sun.

Like a blossoming flower kissed by the sun's golden ray,
Each petal is a reminder of joy's bright display.
No longer does comfort reside in night's embrace,
His heart is now free, basking in the light's trace.

The hidden sun now bathes the world in its tender glow,
His spirit ascends high, a radiant inner show.
No more clouds to obscure the boundless sky,
His spirit is pure, as hope takes flight up high.

His life, a thriving garden adorned with grace,
In this bloom of joy, a smile graces his face.
Where once he would falter, now he firmly stands,
In this vibrant bloom of joy, hope expands in grand.

"Ripple of Positivity"

Ripples of positivity from his heart freely flow,
Spreading like the wind, a vibrant, hopeful glow.
No longer does a frown upon his face abide,
Each ripple is a reminder of life's blessings, far and wide.

Gone are the days of dwelling in the past's disdain,
He now shares positivity, breaking cynicism's chain.
A world once divided now finds unity and grace,
No longer the apathy that once marked the space.

In these ripples, seeds of positivity are sown,
His life, like a garden with hope, has grown.
A radiant spirit, shining through the darkest hours,
No more wallowing; he finds hope in life's flowers.

"Rekindled Connections"

Reunited in the warmth of friendship's embrace,
He discovers a world of connections, a cherished place.
No more isolation, no loneliness to confide,
With bonds that grow deeper, heart and soul coincide.

Each memory, each laugh, each trusted hand,
A testament to the strength of this loving band.
No more solitude as in days long bygone,
No more drifting hearts, no more feeling withdrawn.

The circle of life comes full, as it tends to do,
Joy runs deep in this love, forever true.
Even in the darkest of hours, where he once would reside,
With these friends reunited, he finds hope as his guide.

"Embrace of Serenity"

In the arms of serenity, he discovers his grace,
Like a gentle breeze, a soothing, warm embrace.
No more turmoil to fill his weary soul's role,
In this serenity, he feels complete and whole.

Each moment in this tranquil, hallowed space,
A testament to inner peace's gentle embrace.
No more chaos to encircle his being's core,
In this serenity, he finds healing, evermore.

The tempests that once raged with force untamed,
Now tranquil and calm, reconciled, trained.
No more lingering battles to endure and fight,
In this serenity, his spirit soars, taking flight.

His life unfolds within this tender, warm embrace,
Defined by the peace he's come to eagerly place.
Even in the darkest of hours, where once he would grope,
In this serenity, he discovers boundless hope.

"Journey's End"

He sought a place where healing might reside,
A finish line where pain would finally subside.
Yet time has unveiled a truth so profound,
Healing is a journey where strength is found.

Every step he took, each lesson, each turn,
Challenges embraced, and wisdom to discern.
No comfort is found in that elusive line,
Healing's a journey where his soul shall shine.

The road, once daunting, now his chosen way,
In this path of healing, he finds his day.
No need to evade what lies deep within,
For healing is a journey where life begins.

His life unfolds like a winding road,
With twists and turns, sometimes a heavy load.
But in this journey of healing, he's found his scope,
It's not in the ending, but the journey itself where there's hope.

For healing is a journey that never truly ends,
A path where hearts and spirits make amends.
With each step he takes, he finds his way,
In the ongoing journey of healing each day.

"Emerge from Silence"

From the depths of silence, he embarks to ascend,
Emerging from the abyss, one step, one trend.
His heart, on the mend, begins to raise its voice,
No more emptiness to stifle, no more to constrict its choice.

This emergence from silence, a resolute decree,
Where he finds his voice and sets his spirit free.
Every sound, every melody, laughter, and song,
A testament to the strength that's been growing strong.

No longer does comfort reside in the stifling hush,
This time, he's breaking free from silence's clutch.
The world, once so muted, now echoes with joy,
His spirit reawakened, no longer its employ.

No more shadows to conceal, he steps into the light,
In this newfound time, he'll take an unfettered flight.
His life, like a symphony, begins to ascend,
This time, he surrenders; he'll no longer pretend.

Even in the darkest hours, where he once would grope,
This time, from the silence, he finds endless hope.

"Harmony Restored"

Like a broken chord, once fragmented, now restored,
His life found peace as harmony was explored.
No more discord, no more inner divide,
In this newfound harmony, he'd learn to reside.

Every note, every moment, each lesson, each grace,
A testament to the journey he'd willingly embrace.
No more chaos, no more despair's cruel art,
In this newfound harmony, he'd mend his heart.

The melodies, once fractured, now entwine,
In this harmony, his spirit begins to brightly shine.
No more discord, no more confusion's chain,
In this newfound harmony, he'd break free from the pain.

His life, like a symphony, resounding and grand,
Full of energy, joyous moments, and dreams to understand.
For even in the darkest hours, where he once tried to cope,
In this newfound harmony, he'd find enduring hope.

"Horizon of Hope"

His hope takes flight, a soaring, vivid sight,
In the boundless horizon, radiant and bright,
No more the shadows of a burdened past,
No longer donning a frown, he's found his cast.

He'll ride the tide with dreams that reach the sky,
The distance that once loomed, now a gleam in his eye,
A world of possibilities, no room for doubt,
Fear has no place; his spirit sings and shouts.

The burdens that once anchored him, they're gone,
In this newfound freedom, he'll journey on,
His life, a vast expanse, a landscape wide,
With pride, he strides; let hope be his guide.

Even in the darkest hours, where once he'd grope,
He's found within himself enduring hope.

"Breaking the Cycle"

In shadows deep, a soul did sway,
Caught in a cycle, day by day.
Depression's grip, relentless hold,
A tale of sorrow, often told.

Yet deep within, a spark remained,
A spirit strong, though often pained.
He broke despair, found inner might,
To chase his dreams, dispel the night.

With courage from depths, he'd rise above,
In written words, he found self-love.
In wisdom's grace, he broke despair,
Found happiness beyond compare.

This tale, a lesson for us all,
With inner strength, we can stand tall.
In shadows' grasp, we'll find the way,
To brighter skies, from night to day.

About the Author

Jesse Adams is a passionate poet whose words breathe life into emotions and experiences. With a unique ability to craft verses that resonate with the soul, Jesse's poetry invites readers into a world of vivid imagery and profound reflection. Through the art of poetry, Jesse weaves stories and sentiments that capture the essence of human existence, leaving an indelible mark on those who venture into the lyrical landscapes of his work.

When he's not writing he can be found drawing, painting, making music or watching horror movies.

Made in the USA
Columbia, SC
30 September 2023